Conscious Parents, Conscious Kids

Conscious Parents, Conscious Kids

◆ ◆ ◆

**100% of the proceeds of this book
will go directly towards
the Access True Knowledge Foundation**

Access LLC
www.accessconsciousness.com

Conscious Parents,
Conscious Kids

Published by Access LLC
www.accessconsciousness.com

ISBN: 978-0-9775146-8-7

Printed and Bound by Watson Ferguson & Company Unit 1/655
Toohey Road, Salisbury 4107

Table of Contents

Prelude

Conscious Parents, Conscious Kids is a global initiative for parenting with conscious awareness. It is about people who have created a conscious environment and an extraordinary life for their children and themselves.

This collection of anecdotes and narratives comes from children and parents immersed in living with conscious awareness. Because *Conscious Parents, Conscious Kids* is dedicated to kids, it also features inspiration and helpful tips for kids from kids.

These articles vary widely in content and style. Some capture a moment in time, some offer insights and others reflect people's choices about how to live their lives. Instead of lecturing you or telling you "how to," we hope these stories will awaken your awareness and lighten your spirit.

What are the infinite possibilities that they will inspire you to create a conscious space that allows all of life to come to you with ease and joy and glory?

The Target of This Book

Conscious Parents, Conscious Kids is about helping parents and kids to be in oneness and consciousness. Consciousness is the awareness, the perception, the receiving and the being of all things without judgment. This book is not about teaching, proving or instructing; it is about facilitating greater awareness of what is possible for you and your kids.

What are the infinite possibilities that this book will provide valuable insights and inspiration to raise your awareness so you can make parenting with your kids more conscious and enjoyable?

The information contained in this book is based on the Access Energy for Transformation way of being.

There is also a *Conscious Parents, Conscious Kids* website, which includes podcasts (short audio programs) that provide inspirational anecdotes about parents who have created a conscious environment and an extraordinary life for their children and themselves. This website has been created and constructed to become a global information resource for parents, extended family, children and people who work with children. The website address is www.accessconsciouskids.com

We hope you enjoy both the book and the website.

What else is possible?

With Greatest Gratitude
Chutisa and Steven Bowman

♦ ♦ ♦

100% of the proceeds of this book will go directly towards the Access True Knowledge Foundation

Foreword

This book is a gift to our children. It shows parents that there is a way to support kids in having fun and being themselves, no matter what that looks like, and it acknowledges children for their talents and abilities in so many areas that may not have been acknowledged before.

I would like to thank Chutisa and Steve Bowman for collaborating with so many people to create this book and for compiling all the amazing, inspiring and expansive stories from people around the world who use the tools of Access Energy Transformation to make positive choices in their lives.

I wish to express my gratitude to all the people who have contributed their wonderful stories to this project. (There is a list of contributors at the back of this book.) Without you this book would not exist. And to Dona Haber, for her gift of editing.

I would also like to thank Gary Douglas, the founder of Access, and Dr. Dain Heer for their continuous, patient contribution to so many people across the world, for their work to increase consciousness on this planet and for their vision of Access True Knowledge Schools, which we hope will be created in the very near future. Schools that will empower kids to know what they know. A very different reality.

Ease, Joy and Glory

Simone Milasas
World Wide Coordinator Access Energy Transformation

♦   ♦   ♦

Wouldn't it be great if you could
create the space that allowed your kids to
unleash their potential and burst through
the limitations that hold them back?
To create ease, joy and glory in
everything they do and to consciously
take charge of their own life?

Everything Is Choice!

Everything Is Infinite Possibility!

The Five Elements
of Conscious Parenting
by Chutisa Bowman

Can you imagine what it would be like to raise conscious and aware children?

Conventional parenting is often based on a philosophy which encourages parents to stop listening to what they instinctively know is essential for their child's development of awareness. Most parents believe that they are in charge of their children and must be in command of their children's life. They often demand obedience from their children. Are you one of these parents? Do you have the point of view that parenting is about discipline, conformity, consistency and control? Do you have the judgment that parenting is too serious to have fun with?

As a transpersonal counselor, I have observed that when children are tightly controlled, directed and disciplined with force and effort, they close up. They cut off. When parents attempt to raise children to be normal, real and predictable, they impose huge limitations and judgments on them. They do not encourage and allow for the greatness of their children. Somewhere along the way, children learn that their own knowing, perceiving and awareness are not important and so they stop having them. The good news is that it doesn't have to be this way! As parents we can choose to change this unconscious way of parenting that has been carried on for generations.

When I speak of conscious parenting, I am not talking about learning new techniques to modify children's behavior, communicate with them or build their self-esteem. While these techniques are useful, they are for the most part directed at changing the behavior of children! My point of view about conscious parenting is different. It is not about changing the child. It is about embracing a new way of parenting from conscious awareness. This has an amazing positive effect on a child!

When my daughter, Sharidan, was going through her teenage years, I became aware that the way for me to parent her with ease and joy was to function with total awareness and cultivate true communion and closeness with her. To do this, I put into practice the five elements of conscious parenting: honor, trust, allowance, vulnerability, and gratitude. I cultivated closeness by creating a conscious bond with her, by being vulnerable, by trusting her, by being in allowance of her (instead of judging her), by honoring her and having gratitude for her. No matter what she chose or had chosen, no matter what she was doing or had done.

I learned about the five elements for creating great closeness with my daughter from Gary Douglas, the founder of Access Energy for Transformation.

Gary exemplified the way becoming a conscious parent begins by being conscious and aware in every way. The most amazing conscious parenting bond I have ever seen was between Gary and his daughter, Grace. The energy that flows between them is extraordinarily remarkable.

◆ ◆ ◆

Putting the Five Elements of Conscious Parenting into Practice

Honor. The first element for creating communion and great closeness is honor. To honor my daughter, I began by treating her with total regard. I trusted that she had ability to take care of herself and that she would do what was right for her.

Sharidan, for example, is not a morning person. When she gets up in the morning, she prefers to be by herself and move about the house without having to interact with anyone. She couldn't have differed more with my view of being an exuberant expression of life as soon as I wake up. I used to try to cajole her into becoming energetic in the morning. This annoyed her immensely. But once I put the five elements of conscious parenting into practice, I began to honor Sharidan's way of being. I stopped irritating her with my early morning repartee and enthusiastic chitchat.

More importantly, I stopped expecting her to change her viewpoints so that she would experience life the same way I experienced it. I only interacted with her in the morning when she initiated it. I allowed her to have her point of view totally. We didn't make one another wrong, and we didn't try to change the other. When I honor Sharidan, I honor myself. When Sharidan honors herself in what she chooses, she honors me.

An additional, very important aspect of honoring my daughter includes honoring myself and not going against what works for me. This means not going against my perceiving, knowing, being or receiving. I don't contract my awareness, ever. I don't divorce, deny or suppress any part of myself. I take care of myself. I am willing to be me, to show up as me and do what is right for me.

By not contracting my awareness around Sharidan, I am able to have infinite communion with her. I can maintain our connection and be aware of her and everything around us. Communion is an awareness of all things. It is the oneness that we all are. To be in communion requires me to be conscious. When I am in communion with all things and particularly with my daughter, the energy I perceive tells me, "Don't go there. Don't do this. Don't tell her what to do." Instead of thinking, "She should do this" or "She should do that," I follow the energy and let the energy facilitate me in what I do.

I stopped trying to be a "good mother" based on the traditional perspective of our society. I became aware that I didn't honor me or my daughter when I bought other people's ideas about what a "good mother" was supposed to be and do. I saw that I was actually divorcing myself when I tried to be a "good mother." I became aware that the conventional model of mother-daughter relationship doesn't actually work for Sharidan and me.

I stopped buying into all the belief systems about what good parenting was supposed to be and stopped assuming or expecting that my daughter had the same belief systems. This was an amazing turning point in our life.

Sharidan is now twenty-one and she has grown into an extraordinary being. We have eliminated the separation between us and created a communion that is a continuous state of expansiveness. We have created a mother-daughter relationship that is out of the ordinary and we are willing to have it be an ever-changing canvas.

Trust. The second element of conscious parenting is trust. Most people have misidentified and misapplied what it means to trust. They think trust means blind faith. Trusting my daughter doesn't mean I allow myself to be unmindful and oblivious to everything that goes on with her. I choose to be intensely aware and trust that she will always do what is best for her.

I don't have blind faith that she is going to be obedient and totally abide by my requests or that she is going to do what I wish. Trust is simply knowing that my daughter is always going to do what she is going to do. Most parents expect their children to do what they want them to do rather than what the children are actually going to do. They expect their children to become who they want them to become, and when this doesn't happen, the parents get angry because they "trusted" that their children would match their personal vision for them. That's not trust. Trust is knowing that one's children are never going to be any different than they are—unless they choose to be.

After I learned about the true meaning of trust, I stopped expecting my daughter to do what I wanted her to do (such as keeping her room clean and tidy). I trusted her to do what she would do. If she was going to leave her room messy and untidy, then I trusted her to do that. If she was going to stay up late at night, I trusted her to do that. Trust was being aware that she is a night owl and knowing that as such, she was going to stay up late.

From my experience "trust" is never taking a fixed point of view about anything my daughter does or doesn't do, or how she is or is not. I don't expect Sharidan to be any different than she is. I wholeheartedly trust her to be who she is and to do what is right for her, and I know that she will always honor me in whatever way she can.

Most importantly, in order to be in this space of trust, I have to sincerely trust me. I have to trust myself enough to know that I know. I trust that I have the ability to access and receive every piece of information I require about everything, including what it takes to be a conscious parent.

For me, trust is about expanding my awareness. Awareness is the capacity to know everything. I know that I can trust Sharidan to be who she is and to do what is right for her. I don't trust her to do what I want her to do. I trust her to do what she will do. If she is going to keep her room in a mess, then I trust her to do that. I don't trust her to comply with my requirement of keeping her room clean. If I do that, I am destroying my own awareness. I am making my decision about what I want to be greater than my awareness of what is.

I also trust that I have the ability to be totally present in my life and in Sharidan's life without any judgment of anything that goes on.

Allowance. Allowance is the third element of conscious parenting. Allowance is allowing things to be as they are. It's the attitude that everything that goes on is just an interesting point of view. I allow everything to be as it is, without resisting and reacting to it—and without aligning and agreeing with it. I don't resist and react to my daughter—nor do I align and agree with her. When I am in allowance, I am in awareness and I don't have to do anything at all. I don't have the need to control her. So what if she wants to reside in a messy bedroom? She'll clean it up sooner or later. So what if she doesn't want to finish her meal? She won't go hungry. This attitude of allowance, all by itself, eliminates most potential conflict in our home.

As soon as I brought allowance into my parenting practice, I was able to see the uniqueness of my daughter's point of view and regard it as just an interesting point of view. I realized there is no such thing as right, wrong, good or bad; everything is just choice. I recognized that what works for me may not work for her and vice versa. When Sharidan chose to go backpacking in India and Southeast Asia with a girl friend at age twenty, I was not the slightest bit excited about her choice. Nevertheless, I did not criticize or pass judgment. Such criticism would have been based on, "I want you to do it my way." That's not allowance.

Even though I did not want her to go backpacking and thought what she was choosing to do was weird, I didn't try to stop her. My attitude was, "If that's what you want to do, go do it." I didn't try to prevent her from being different from me, even though I was not pleased about the places she had chosen to visit. I do not get pleasure from the same things my daughter does, but I do want her to have her own life.

When she announced what she was planning to do, I asked her, "What do you require of me?"

......"To be happy for me please, Mom," she replied.

I became aware that it was more expansive not to resist or react to what she had chosen to do. I also saw that I didn't have to agree or align with it. I simply chose to be happy for her and allow her to have her point of view. I was in allowance of what she was doing and how she was doing it. I allowed her to be everything she is without expecting anything of her or imposing my point of view on her.

I also became aware that in order to be a conscious mother, I had to be in allowance of myself as a mother. I had to be willing to see my viewpoints and ideas about motherhood as just interesting points of view. In the past, I tried to create myself as a "good mother" according to everyone else's point of view. I made being a good mother significant. I used to beat myself up for not being a good mother. Given that I love working and my work required me to travel extensively, people often judged me to be a terrible mother for leaving my daughter. I used to buy their points of view as real and true. I saw that I didn't have to do that.

Now when people's comments, ideas and beliefs come at me, I let them go around me and I am still me. I have stopped buying the idea that other people's beliefs have to affect me. Those are just their points of view. I don't have to resist or react to what they say or do and I don't have to agree or align with it. When I am in allowance, I am in awareness and I don't have to do anything at all. I have a total freedom to be a mother the way that works for Sharidan and me.

Vulnerability. The fourth element of conscious parenting is vulnerability. Vulnerability means being open to receive everything without judgment. There's no barrier, there's no resistance, there's no defense. There is total sensitivity, which means I can receive everything my daughter says and does.

I became aware that in order to create an extraordinary relationship with Sharidan, I had to see where I was putting up automatic barriers and start pushing them down. Once I learned about vulnerability, I made a demand of myself, "I choose to be vulnerable no matter what. No barriers." I chose to just be there as I am. Whenever I became aware of potential disagreement or a likely conflict between Sharidan and me, I would become aware of the barriers that came up and I would immediately push them down. I adopted the attitude that she was just expressing her point of view at the moment, and I would be receptive to it. I noticed that when I did this, I started to have a sense of connection and communication with my daughter.

I found that when I pushed my barriers down and became willing to receive everything without judgment, I could actually be present for Sharidan and we could have a communication about the subject. True communication could not occur as long as I was doing barriers.

Every time my daughter experienced frustration over challenging circumstances, I would become vulnerable, let the barriers down and allow her to vent her frustration and concern. I simply listened and allowed her to figure out what was best for her. I noticed that whenever I forgot to be vulnerable, I tried to be a "wise" and "responsible" mother and I forced my points of view, concepts and ideas on her. When I did this, I interfered with her self-discovery. Worse, I often completely missed the boat and got bogged down in my own opinions and points of view of the world.

I discovered that willingness to be vulnerable with myself as a mother was vital if I wanted to create a harmonious bond with Sharidan. The paradox of being vulnerable is that it also required me to be willing to receive everything without judgment. Being vulnerable took a great deal of willingness to let go of the old notion of being in control. To receive everything without judgment, I had to be willing to let go of the illusion that I could be in control.

I have made the willingness to receive everything without judgment the guiding principle in my life. I practice it in my way of being with my daughter, with my husband and in my work. If I am experiencing a limitation or difficulty in my life, whether it has to do with my interactions with Sharidan or with my husband, I know that there has to be something that I am not willing to receive. I have learned that if anything in my life is not working, it is because I am unwilling to perceive, know, be or receive something. I am not being vulnerable. When I notice that I feel anxious and tense, I make it a practice to become more vulnerable and receptive and to push down any barriers. When I catch myself in the act of resisting or reacting to something, I ask myself this question: "What am I unwilling to receive here?"

The practice of being vulnerable allows me to be present with Sharidan. It also allows me to know that I don't have to be a perfect mother for her. I can be vulnerable with the places I'm not perfect. I can be willing to change. I don't have to judge myself for not being perfect or for not being where I would like to be. Being vulnerable allows both Sharidan and me to create a communion that is a continuous state of expansiveness.

Gratitude. The final element of conscious parenting is gratitude. Gratitude is not just a response to attaining something we desire or expect; it is a state of beingness. Gratitude is about being and embodying a sense of appreciation and thankfulness. When I am in gratitude, I am grateful for everything that my daughter is, with no expectation or judgment. I am grateful to have her in my life just as she chooses to be. I am grateful for who she is. I am grateful for the fact that I am her mother.

Gratitude expects nothing. It requires nothing. I became aware that whenever I looked for rightness or wrongness, I was not being grateful. Rightness and wrongness preclude gratitude because they are judgments, and gratitude and judgment cannot exist in the same universe. The more I let go of my expectations, projections and judgments, the more gratitude I have for who my daughter is and what she does. I see clearly what a gift she is.

The Joy of Conscious Parenting

The practice of these five elements of conscious parenting has transformed the way I function as a mother and changed the way Sharidan and I communicate and relate with each other. These five elements have also provided infinite possibilities for my own personal evolution. They have also enhanced my relationship with my daughter and expanded the consciousness for our whole family.

The short stories in this book offer many points of view and inspiration about conscious parenting. They illustrate the way parents have incorporated honor, trust, allowance, vulnerability and gratitude into their lives to create communion with their children. This is not a book of theory, hypothesis or logical reasoning about parenting. Instead of teaching or lecturing about how important it is to be a conscious parent, we have chosen to tell some inspirational true stories instead. These stories paint an exceptional picture of what is possible for parents and children.

While reading this book, we invite you to identify which of the five elements are represented in each of the stories, and how these may create for you the joy of conscious parenting.

Parenting Is Not About Ownership and Control

by Gary Douglas

Most parents think that parenting is about ownership and control. They believe they have total control of their children's lives and who their children become when they grow up. The idea that parents are—or are supposed to be—in control of their children and what they do is a major misconception and leads parents to misidentify what their job is.

The truth is that parents aren't in control. It's actually the other way around. Kids are in control of themselves. Kids choose who they are going to have as parents! We don't choose them; they choose us. Children come in to this life with a point of view and a job to do. They choose us because we somehow fit in with their plan.

I was born into a family that was "normal, average, and real." In my family, we were supposed to live a normal, average life. We were not supposed to be extraordinary in any way. When I expressed interest in art, music and literature, they thought I was weird. They did nothing to encourage that, and in fact, did everything they could to discourage those interests and show me that I was wrong. They took me to lots of movies to get me to look at average stuff, cowboy movies, in particular. They wanted me to get clear that my interest in art, music and literature was leading me in the wrong direction. Of course, that didn't work. And today I am one of the weirdest, wildest, wackiest guys on the planet. It's what I chose. They could never have made me choose their way of being.

Most people have the idea that good parenting is based on being right versus being wrong. They think it's about getting "results," being in control and having all the answers. They think good parenting is about indoctrinating kids into a certain way of being and trying to make life predictable. The problem with trying to train kids to be normal, real, and predictable is that it imposes huge limitations and judgments on them. It does not encourage and allow for the greatness of children.

The truth is your kids are not limited, normal, average and predictable. They are magic. Their magic is their infinite beingness. Would you be willing to claim, own, and acknowledge that your children have magic within them?

> *What kind of possibilities can you create today? What else is possible?*

Are You Willing to See Your Kids as Infinite Beings?

by Dr. Dain Heer

Are you willing to see your kids as infinite beings? Would you be willing to acknowledge that babies come in to this world aware? Kids come into this life with total awareness. Have you ever seen a baby scream at just the right pitch to drive nails between your eyes? How do they know to use that particular pitch every time they want something? They are aware. They know exactly the right pitch to make you run like crazy to pick them up or do what they want.

People say, "Yes, but they're just babies!" That isn't quite right. They may have baby bodies, but they are also infinite beings with infinite awareness. Children are big beings with little bodies. If we would actually treat them that way and acknowledge the awareness that they have from the youngest age, we could support, facilitate and allow that awareness to show up in their lives.

As an infinite being, is there anything you wouldn't know? No. You know everything. Is there anything you wouldn't be able to receive? No. You are able to receive everything.

Please recognize that infinite beings can be wonderful, kind and generous, but they can also choose to be mean and awful and break everything in your house. Seeing your kids as infinite beings doesn't mean that you believe everything they do is wonderful, saintly and oriented for greatness.

One of the greatest lies of parenthood is that of a sudden, at some point in their late teens, children finally become beings unto themselves. This is usually around sixteen or eighteen, depending on the country you live in. But the truth is, there is no magic day when children become full beings. They are full beings even before their bodies are conceived. They are full-on infinite beings throughout their entire lives. If parents would acknowledge that, perhaps we could create a change in the way parenting is done here on Planet Earth.

> *The greatest power is the ability to change, transform and choose.*

Are You Parenting Just Like Your Mum and Dad?

by Gary Douglas

A lot of parents assume that their children are going to have a better life than they had. They try to create something different for their children than what was created for them. Often they make decisions about what was wrong with the way they were parented and then try to create a parenting system that's different from what was given to them. Usually they go overboard in the opposite direction, which doesn't accomplish anything, except to wrap the same insanity in a slightly different package.

I remember a time I walked into the living room about two a.m. and found my oldest son watching television. I said, "Young man, don't you realize you have to get up and go to work in the morning? It's two o'clock in the morning, and you should be going to bed!"

All of a sudden, I heard my mother's words coming out of my mouth. I was speaking exactly the same words she had spoken to me when I was that age.

I realized that when I was my son's age, I wasn't any better about going to bed early than he was going to be, so I said, "Never mind. I didn't listen to my mom, and you're not going to listen to me. Good night."

I was willing to hear myself speaking as my mother and to see that I was unconsciously trying to duplicate the way she had raised me. I knew my son was not going to listen to me any more than I listened to my mom.

I was willing to ask myself, "Is it worthwhile for me to try to control this child? Or do I have to see that he's going to choose for himself, regardless of my furious attempts at control?"

When you notice yourself imposing control and limitations on your kids or trying to parent them the way you were parented, you can say, "Oops!" then destroy and uncreate whatever it was you were doing and choose again. Are you willing to give up your fixed points of view of what parenting has to look like?"

Would you be willing to relate to life in spontaneous interaction with the energy of the moment, without thought, intention, desire or consideration of the next moment?

What Does Consciousness Mean ... Exactly?

by Nancy O'Connor

Raising a conscious child requires that we perceive the magic children see, and acknowledge it as real, not imaginary. As adults, most of us have lost the ability to wonder. This is truly unfortunate, because it is this sense of wonder that leads us to ask questions and become aware of the infinite possibilities all around us. Our children are already there. Our children look at life and wonder, "What is possible?" Do you ever ask yourself this question?

Often, as adults, we try to figure things out. We use our limited minds to find answers rather than using our unlimited awareness to see the infinite possibilities. We don't realize that our answers provide us with a lifetime of limitations to overcome. We get stuck and think, "It's either this or this." "I can do this—I can't do this." "I can be this—I can't be this." Children don't live in these limitations.

What does consciousness mean exactly? For many, it may imply the attainment of some sort of spiritual superiority. For me, it is about an awareness that is so intense I become oneness with all things, separate from nothing. Superiority can't exist in this place. Nothing is excluded. Everything is beautiful: the good, the bad and the ugly. I call this the insane beauty in which everything has its own perfection. My child has been a great gift in showing me this insane beauty as it exists every day, hidden in moments that are easy to disregard or judge as wrong, from the spilled milk and broken glass on the floor to the spider's web in a corner or the dog's poop on the sidewalk.

True visionaries in every field have managed to see beyond the limitations we assume are real and set in place. Picasso said he spent all of his life learning again to see as a child.

What would it take for us to consider a new way of being with our children that is not about imposing our limitations and judgments but offers instead questions that will empower them to choose to know what they already know?

> ### *The journey to raising a conscious child begins with a question.*

Conscious Parents Ask Questions
by Glenna Rice

Conscious and aware kids create ease and joy for their parents, and conscious, aware parents create ease and joy for their children. The more awareness you, as a parent, can facilitate in a family, the more joy and ease everyone receives. The more Access tools my children learn, the easier it becomes to create my life. And a parent wouldn't want more ease for what reason?

How do you create more ease as a parent? You ask questions. You become a walking question. You ask your children things like, "Is there something else you could choose?" "What else is possible?" "Is there another way you could be with this?" "Hey kids, this doesn't work for me. What else is possible?" Once you start asking, you—and your children—begin to receive information and difficult situations begin to change.

Children are brilliant. They want to make us happy and they have so much awareness and knowing to gift us. Everything can change when we stop parenting from limitation and begin to ask kids what they know that we don't know, that if we did, would change our lives and create an extraordinary family.

When you, as a parent, are willing to always be in the question with your children, you find ways of handling things with greater ease. When you ask questions, situations don't feel solid, heavy and hopeless. No issue or problem seems too big to solve.

You start to have more allowance for your children, for your skills as a parent and for yourself. Things that were significant and troubling start to barely even faze you.

One of the many great questions I have been asked is, "What if having children is part of creating an extraordinary life?" It has become one of the many questions I use to create my family and my life.

> ### *Everything is the question, nothing is the answer.*

Treat Your Children the Way You Should Have Been Treated

by Dr. Dain Heer

I had just gotten a cool, new television set with a surround-sound speaker. I'd had it for a couple of days and I was still trying to figure out how to operate it when Gary's daughter Grace asked me if she could watch it.

I said, "Yeah, you can watch it, but just this once."

I heard the words coming out of my mouth and was shocked by what I heard myself saying. I didn't like the way it felt—or the way it sounded. I didn't like the energy it created. I asked, "Who is saying those words that just came out of my mouth?" They were completely inappropriate to the situation.

Grace, at age nineteen, was more aware of other people and their things than anyone else I know, regardless of their age. She would not abuse other people or their property. For me to make a comment like that was really out of place.

I felt crappy about what I had said. I went to Gary and asked, "Can you help me with this?"

Gary asked, "Were you responsible as a kid? Did you take care of other people's stuff?" ... I said, "Yeah. Of course."

Then he asked me, "What if you were to treat Grace the way you *should* have been treated as a kid, instead of the way you *were* treated?"

I said, "Whoa!" I immediately recognized that I had a stepmother who didn't trust me. She didn't see that even as a very young kid, I took care of her possessions, my dad's possessions and my own possessions.

My stepmother's point of view was, "Children can't be trusted. They won't take care of anything. You have to control them or they will destroy everything." This was the viewpoint she had grown up with and this was the point of view she imposed on me. She didn't have any awareness of me, nor was she willing to see who I really was. And here I was, doing the same thing to Grace.

Fortunately, with Gary's help, I saw this. I was willing to look at myself and ask, "What point of view do I have that creates this limitation and what would it take to get rid of it?"

Like my stepmother, most parents tend to impose their point of view on their kids. They never actually look at their children and see who they are.

What would it be like to look at kids as individuals? No two of them are alike. So how could you apply the same rules and the same way of parenting to all of them? You have to treat them as individuals. You have to see what they're capable of and what they're not capable of. If you create as few rules as you possibly can, then they don't have to break so many.

To raise kids with conscious awareness, you have to be willing to give up your fixed points of view of what good parenting is. You have to be willing to give up thinking you know the way things are supposed to be and what they're supposed to look like. The key word is *willingness*. Willingness means by choice and without reluctance.

Would you be willing to have a look at everything that comes out of your mouth and everything that's going on in your head and ask, "Okay, is this truth? Does this make me feel light?" If it doesn't make you feel light, there's something about it that's not true.

Be willing to look at yourself and the way you are parenting your kids. Ask "What point of view do I have that is creating this limitation and what would it take to get rid of it?" Then you can change it.

How does it get any better than this?

They Told Me That Newborn Babies Don't Smile

by Nancy O'Connor

When my son Calder was born, he was placed in my arms and he smiled. We have all been told the story, "Newborn babies don't smile. It must be gas." But I have a photo to prove it: Calder smiled.

So began the first of many questions I asked as a parent. How did it happen that Calder smiled? Did he already know me?

As an artist, I live in the question and I never assume that anything is as it appears to be. This has been an invaluable tool for me as a parent. My investigative mind seems a compulsive annoyance to many people except other artists and creative thinkers. Very few people value the question. They think the most important thing on this planet is to find the answer.

As a new parent, I attempted to follow this line of reasoning about taking care of my infant son. I read book after book after book on child rearing, trying to find the answers to a million questions. But the "answers" just never seemed to apply.

Book after book gave charts and formulas for the "proper" development in children. Immediate alarm was signaled if one's child didn't match the charts. There was a "solution" for every problem, an answer.

Calder, of course, didn't match the charts, and I soon realized that child rearing according to these rules was going to be a long, tedious and unhappy job. These "rules" seemed set in stone and I feared that if I didn't follow them, my child would turn out to be a deviant monster. If I was not utterly vigilant, disaster would surely strike. I began taking antidepressants. They didn't work.

Finally, out of desperation, I resorted to doing what I do best. I had been trained as a documentary photographer and video artist. I picked up my video camera and began to film everything about Calder. I began observing what he was doing and asking questions. Who knew that my professional training would provide such a valuable parenting tool? All assumptions and fixed points of view had to be put aside. I simply followed the energy of whatever was going on.

My observations led me to realize that an amazing being inhabited Calder's little body. I stopped assuming that he didn't know exactly what I was saying to him. Although words were not yet available for him to use in response to me, the energy was, and he was communicating just as stridently as if he'd had words. We were communicating through a language of energy that in many ways is much more complex than words.

On realizing this, I began to speak with Calder in a very different way. I addressed him not as a baby, but as a being who could know, perceive and receive exactly what I was saying. This was not linear communication; it was energetic. It was beautiful, clear and strong. Every parent has experienced it and perhaps disregarded the gift of it.

Just as I had accepted Calder's smile when he was born, I came to accept the gift of our communication long before he spoke his first words.

Be you—and change the world.
Be not you—and suffer the world.

Allow Children to Be Who They Are Every Step of the Way

by Gary Douglas

As parents we tend to make many decisions and judgments about our kids that limit what our children can actually become. Rather than living in the moment with their kids, many parents buy into the conventional model of parenting. They try to create a plan and a system for their children's future that will handle everything forever. They think that if they make the "right" choice or decision for their children, it will handle everything forever.

If you want to become a conscious parent, you have to be willing to erase all of your ideas about what you think your child must be.

When my youngest son was a baby, I decided that he was Jesus Christ incarnate. Of course, that wasn't true. He's a carpenter, but that's about the only place Jesus Christ and he cross paths. At some point, I had to look at him and ask, "Is he really the next Messiah or is he just a kid?" Unfortunately a lot of us think our sons and daughters are perfect and they're going to become something great. If they don't do something "great," we begin to get disappointed. We judge ourselves or we judge our kids, either of which creates a sense of separation.

It's important to recognize that your kids are who your kids are. It's not about what you want them to be, what you think they ought to be or what you think they can be. You have to see them for who they are. It's not up to you to determine who they are. That's up to them, no matter how much you like or dislike their choices.

Children actually choose who they are going to be before they are born. My daughter Grace definitely chose to wear designer fashion before she came in to this life. At her first birthday party, she threw down the toys she had been given and picked up the dresses. She held them against her body to show us what they would look like. She was one year old, and she has continued to love fashion and fine clothes all her life.

Please recognize that who your children are is who they choose to be. If we, as parents, can have that without judging it as right, wrong, good or bad, we allow them to step into everything that's possible for them. As long as we have a judgment about what is good and what is bad, we limit what is possible. If we don't judge our kids, we allow them to be who they are every step of the way.

I would like my youngest son to choose more than he has. Is he choosing more? No. Is he working hard? Yes. Is he enjoying his kids? Yes. Is he happy?

Mostly. But I'm not the determinant of that. He is. He has to create his life. I can't do it for him.

When I was a kid, people would say to me, "What do you want to be when you grow up?"

I'd say, "Happy."

And they'd say, "No son, what do you want to be when you grow up?"

"Happy."

"No, no. Do you want to be a doctor, a lawyer, or an Indian chief?"

I'd say, "Yeah, as long as I'm happy." For me, happiness was the target in life, not money, not success. None of those things.

And it's what I want for my kids, too. The only thing I want is for them to be happy—to be joyful.

Define nothing and be aware of everything.

Being in Allowance

by Claudia Cano

My son, Alejandro, an amazing being in a six-year-old body, started "playing" with an older kid during a class I was attending. I could clearly see that the other kid wasn't playing with Alejandro; he was hurting him—and enjoying it. I called Alejandro over and asked him, "Alejandro, is this kid playing with you or is he hurting you and enjoying it?"

He looked straight into my eyes and said, "Hurting me!"

I said, "Okay, so why would you choose to play with him?"

He answered, "Because I like it!" That was an answer I wasn't expecting! I mean, who in his right mind would enjoy being hurt?

So, I said, "Okay," and Alejandro returned to his "game."

I'm not going to lie. I was furious! How could my son enjoy being hurt by this kid? Then I noticed that the angrier I got, the harder the other kid hit him. Suddenly I realized that playing this game was Alejandro's choice and that resisting and reacting to it was only making things worse. He was willingly choosing to be hurt, whether I liked it or not, and the only thing I could do was to be in allowance of his choice.

I started destroying and uncreating all the points of view I had aligned and agreed with and resisted and reacted to in connection with his choice. It was hard for me to do that while watching the kid hurt Alex. At first I had to turn my head away as I destroyed and uncreated my viewpoints about what he was doing. Eventually I knew I was in allowance, because Alex's choice became just an interesting point of view. I was no longer resisting and reacting to it.

When the class was over, we got into the car and I saw that Alex had the beginnings of a black eye and some bruises. I wasn't angry or sad. It was just interesting. I asked him, "How was it?" He said, "It was good!" "Did you enjoy it?" "Yes!"

I asked, "How does it get any better than this?" and "What else is possible?" Five minutes later, he said, "Mommy, could you destroy and uncreate that I like that?"

When we got home he asked me if I could "put my hands" on his body where it was sore. This is an Access tool we use when he hurts himself. I said, "Yes," and the next day there was no sign of bruises.

More important than the lack of bruises, however, was the fact that I had empowered Alex to choose for himself, and he had discovered on his own that letting another kid hurt him wasn't really very much fun after all.

> *Are you willing to be in total allowance, to have no reaction, no resistance, and no alignment or agreement?*

Stop Trying to Live Your Life Through Your Kids

by Dr. Dain Heer

Most parents have high hopes and dreams for their children. Oftentimes, the common thread connecting these hopes and dreams is the idea that the children will grow up to fulfill the parents' own dreams and expectations of success. All parents want their children to grow up to be happy, healthy, and successful. However, some parents expect their children to grow up to be something that they themselves wished to be but were not able to achieve. To some extent, parents transmit these dreams to their children in the form of expectations.

Many parents have the misconception that conveying expectations to children is a way to inspire them or communicate care, support, reassurance, confidence, and value. Unfortunately, expectations can have the opposite effect. Growing up with too many expectations can be devastating to a child. In many cases, the spoken and unspoken expectations communicate a message that is disapproving and critical and what children hear is that they're not good enough.

Even if you don't state your expectations, children pick them up from your non-verbal behavior and energy. They know exactly what you're thinking when they say, "I've decided to go to art school instead of pursuing my pharmacy degree."

What would it be like if you got rid of those expectations?

If you'll get rid of your judgments for what you haven't been able to create in your life, you won't try to project those things onto your kids under the guise that they'll be able to do something greater than you did. You won't try to live your life through your kids or try to get them to succeed because you believe you failed. You'll allow them to choose whatever they choose, in whatever way it shows up for them, without trying to make up for the mistakes you made in your life. And really, if you look at your life, are those "mistakes" actually errors? Or have you created and chosen everything that has shown up in your life just because you have?

What if your life wasn't wrong? What if those things you regret weren't really mistakes? What if your life is just fine the way it is? What if your children know what it would take to create the life they would like to have? What if they could choose something that far surpasses anything you could imagine for them? Would you be willing to allow your children to supersede you?

In eastern Tennessee, they have a saying: "You can't go above your raisin'." When I heard this for the first time, I imagined muffin with a raisin on top, and I wondered, "What the hell is going above your raisin?"

What they actually meant, of course, was that you couldn't do better than your parents did. You're not supposed to be greater than your parents. You can do almost as well as they did, but they're your parents, so don't exceed what they've done. Don't become greater than they are.

As a parent, wouldn't you like to see your child actually achieve something greater than you have?

I'd like to encourage you, as a parent, to support your kids in going above their raisin', whatever that means to them. Become aware of your spoken and unspoken dreams and expectations for your kids. Destroy and uncreate them—or just put them aside. Wouldn't you like to see your children achieve what truly makes their life sing?

> *When you are in a place of no judgment, there is total allowance of all things.*

Let Your Kids Choose the Life They Desire

by Gary Douglas

At one point, after my son had been in a nursery school a while, all the parents got together for Monday night meetings to talk about our children. They talked about acculturating children and how it was important to give dolls to boys and trucks to girls; otherwise we would be stereotyping them. I said, "What are you talking about?"

When my son was six weeks old, he threw himself off my shoulder onto a truck that was on a shelf. I didn't acculturate him. He had teddy bears and plenty of other toys, but when he saw a truck, he was gone. What's he driving today? A big-ass truck! He was into trucks at six weeks old. He knew where he was going.

When he was ten years old, he wanted to do remote-controlled cars. He said, "Dad will you help me?" I had watched a friend who had a son the same age as mine help his boy do a remote-controlled car, and suddenly it became the father's remote-controlled car, not the kid's remote-controlled car.

I said, "Sorry son, I don't know anything about them. You're going to have to figure it out on your own." Within a few months, he was able to change gear ratios, put different transmissions in them and do all kinds of things. He figured it out on his own.

I have friends who say, "Oh, my son just graduated from Harvard. My son just graduated from Yale. What's your son doing?"

I say, "He's being a carpenter and raising a family." I can hear them thinking, "Oh you poor thing." They are proud of their kids for what they have accomplished and ashamed for me that my son chose what he has chosen. But the one thing I know about my kid is that he can create anything he chooses.

When he was eighteen, he decided to become a carpenter. Somebody asked him to build a fence on an incline, and on his own, he figured out how to do it. I know he can figure out anything, if he chooses to do it. Will he change what he creates as his life in the future? Probably. Do I care what he chooses now? No, it's his life. He needs to live it.

When my children were young I never said "no" when they chose something. The only thing I did was ask, "Are you sure you want to do this?"

My son said he wanted to play soccer. I asked, "Are you sure you want to do this?" He said, "Yes, Dad, I really want to do this." I said, "Okay, fine."

If kids make a commitment to do something, then they'll keep doing it. If you talk them into it (and that's what most parents do) they'll want to quit as soon as it gets tough. But if they have decided they want to do it, then they'll do it. I believe it's important to let kids choose for themselves.

What I wanted my son to do was learn how to ride horses. I bought him a pony. Did he ride the pony? No. Did I buy the pony for him—or for me? Obviously, I bought it for me, because when I was a little boy, I wanted a pony and I didn't get one.

> *Create life as an adventure*
> *instead of an obligation.*

Not from a Place of Imposing Rules

by Dr. Dain Heer

I used to think that the reason I turned out to be well adjusted, somewhat aware and willing to create a life was because of all the rules that were imposed upon me when I was a child.

It's been very interesting for me to observe Gary as he works with his kids. I've known his daughter Grace since she was twelve and I have watched how Gary "parents" her. Over the years, I've noticed that he doesn't impose rules on her.

Gary invites his daughter to have awareness and gives her an opportunity to have everything she can create in the world. He doesn't operate from a place of imposing rules; his parenting comes from being with conscious awareness. Seeing the way Gary is with Grace and the person that she has become has been an amazing gift for me. I've realized the rules parents impose on their children don't create who the children are. The kids already are who they are.

Kids are who they are when they come into this world. They get better or worse, according to their own universe, and the biggest mistake adults make is assuming that children have to be "raised."

As parents, we can influence our children to a certain extent until they are maybe twelve, and then forget it. We can encourage them and educate them a little bit. We have to be aware for them, and we have to let them know what the results of some of their actions are going to be, and then we have to let them choose.

If the encouragement we give them acknowledges who they are, it facilitates their awareness. If it's about helping them acknowledge that they perceive energies, if it's about encouraging them to make choices, then they learn to trust their awareness and see that that have choices. Making choices (like deciding to go to bed at ten instead of staying up until five in the morning) does something positive for them. It makes them feel good and allows them to acknowledge that they have awareness and choice. They're choosing; they aren't just following rules. They see they're making good decisions. Their confidence increases—and their universe expands.

> ### *Choose what you would like to have in your life.*

58

It Was Her Body's Choice

by Julie Tuton & Ron Filson

We wished for a little more ease with parenting our kids and a little less sense of "responsibility." One issue in our family was food. There was always a lot of discussion about what was okay to eat and what was not. Supervising our kids' eating was becoming a full time job, and we were the bad guys, always saying, "No!"

We learned in an Access seminar that we could actually ask our bodies what they wanted to eat and drink and that they would let us know. We could ask, "Body, what would you like to eat?" or "Body, would you like to eat this ___?" and it would answer.

We were excited about the possibilities for reducing disagreements and discussions about food, and taught our kids that they could do this, too. But we weren't sure it would work. Would they really ask their bodies? Would they actually turn down a second piece of chocolate cake because their body said "No"?

One evening at bedtime our seven-year-old daughter Sabrina was standing in the kitchen with the freezer door open, asking if she could have some ice cream.

We replied, "Ask your body." (It wasn't our decision any more!)

Sabrina closed her eyes, became very still, then wrinkled up her nose and said, "Darn!" She closed the freezer and went up to bed.

Success! We were no longer responsible for deciding what she could and could not eat. It was her body's choice, and she honored it.

The willingness to perceive and receive yourself differently is the beginning of creating what you truly desire in your life.

Living in Ten-Second Increments

by Gary Douglas

I often talk to people about living in ten-second increments. The idea behind living in ten-second increments is being present for every moment of your life. If you live in ten-second increments, you create being in the present moment. Most people, rather than living in the moment, try to create a plan and a system for the future so it will show up the way they want it. They create the plan and think they don't need to be aware any longer. But there's only one place we can live—and that's right here, right now. Anything else kills you. You don't get to have a life. You miss out your own life.

If you live in ten-second increments, you can start to break down the conditioning that has you figuring things out and planning in advance. You can learn how to choose in each moment. You can't judge in ten seconds because it's here and it's gone. We prolong our agony in life by judging ourselves and trying to fix what we have judged. This is especially true of the way we parent.

When you do something that you think is bad, how long do you punish yourself for it? How long do you obsess about it? Days? Weeks? Months? If you're living in ten-second increments, you can't do that. What if you just said, "Oh, well, I did that for ten seconds, now what would I like to choose?"

If you practice the art of choosing your life in ten-second increments, you will begin to create choice and infinite opportunity. Most of us parent out of a sense of obligation. We say, "I've got to do this, and I've got to do this, and I've got to do this." But are those things we'd truly like to do? Usually not, but we keep choosing them. Why? Because we think we have to. We think we're obligated to do them and that if we don't, we're bad parents.

When you live in ten-second increments, you get to choose and then choose again. You don't have to stay stuck bad decisions—or good decisions.

> *When you practice the art of choosing your life in ten second increments, you will begin to create choice and the opportunity to receive infinite possibility.*

Live with Your Kids Moment by Moment

by Gary Douglas

There is a lot of psychobabble about positive parenting. Like if you see your children as wonderful, then you create the space for them to go into being wonderful. If you see your children as horrible brats, then you create the space for that. It's like "The Secret" of parenting—what you focus on is what you get.

From my point of view, it's preferable not to focus on anything. I live with my kids moment by moment. This is a bizarre idea for many parents, but ultimately it works. To do this, you have to take each event in life separately. People try to create a system by which they govern their parenting so they are always consistent. But are any two days the same? No. Do any two kids react the same? No. Does your child react the same way every day? No. Do you ever act the same way two days in a row? Or do you change all the time? And when somebody tries to put you in a place where they expect you to respond the same way twice in a row, do you resist and react to that?

When you have a fixed point of view or an expectation about how your children should behave and act, how much freedom does it give them? It doesn't give them any, because your expectation defines their choice. When parents put their points of view on their kids—"John's going to react this way" or "Suzy's going to react that way"—they limit the kids' choices.

When parents have expectations, kids have to either align and agree with their parents' expectations and do what they're expected to do, or they have to resist and react to their expectations and do the opposite. The children don't have the freedom to be who they are.

Try living with your kids moment by moment. Destroy and uncreate your expectations, decisions and judgments, and instead take each event in life separately. Live in ten-second increments.

Ultimately, isn't what you want for your children for them to be who they are, regardless of whether you agree with it or not?

Ask for the greatness of your life.

The Value of Asking a Question

by Nancy O'Connor

My son Calder began walking and talking very early. People would come up to me and comment about how "bright" he was. I had no reference points and didn't wish to develop any. The books, the charts and other advice to parents seemed to lead away from being present and aware with what was occurring right in front of me with my child.

All was not blissful, however. Calder was a dreaded biter. His preschool was threatening to expel him. They said it was very "unusual" for a child with such advanced language skills to bite. Expelled from preschool? I panicked and reverted to reading books and "advice" from other parents, teachers and pediatricians. I lost all my questions. "Advice" poured in from all directions. I tried it all. I removed toys, enforced time outs and demanded he stop the behavior. One morning as I was getting out of the shower Calder snuck up behind me and bit me hard on my rear end. I saw stars, wheeled around and bit him back. We both cried. Nothing worked. His room looked like a monastery—minimal furniture and almost all his toys taken away.

Finally, in frustration and completely at wits end, I decided to observe and wait. It was like waiting for a rattlesnake to strike. Finally it happened; Calder bit a neighbor kid. It took all I had to remain calm. Calder started crying and apologizing as I took him aside.

"Calder," I asked, "What is going on here? What is the reason for your continuing to bite people?" His reply was calm and well considered. "Mama," he said, "there are three stages, first stage: frustration, second stage: anger, third stage: bite!"

At this, I simply had to get up and walk around for a moment. After collecting myself, I went back to him and said, "Okay, fine. You have to stop after stage two." He never bit again.

I tell this story because it made me realize the value of asking a question. Simply and calmly asking the reason why he continued to bite others allowed him to look at his behavior in a different way and to shift it. The question created a space for change and allowed me to see that I had been looking outside of myself for answers rather than asking questions and observing the situation without assumptions or judgments.

> ### *Be you. You are the gift.*

Encourage Awareness Rather Than Making Rules

by Gary Douglas

When my youngest son was about six months old, he would stand in the shopping cart when we went to the store. He always insisted on standing, rather than sitting in the little seats. One day we were at the store and he was standing in the cart and I said, "Young man, you'd better sit down, because if you fall on this concrete floor, it's going to hurt your head. It's going to break your head and it's not going to feel good, so you'd better consider the possibility of sitting down."

He looked at me and sat down. An old lady next to me was horrified and said, "I can't believe anyone would talk to a kid like that." I said, "Why? He's a big being with a small body. He understands what I'm saying."

When you treat your kids as though they know what you're saying, they know what you're saying. Sometimes they may not understand the words and you can give them pictures of what will happen. Sometimes you communicate with them telepathically.

These things are possible and yet many parents will not allow these possibilities into their awareness. Can you imagine how many possibilities parents cut out of their awareness when they buy into the limited perspective of conventional parenting?

I take the approach of asking kids to be aware - not giving them rules. When my kids were little, I would say, "If you touch that stove, it's going to be hot." I wouldn't say, "No, don't touch the stove."

Ultimately "no" becomes a place where you have to be in control of kids, instead of inviting them being in control of themselves. "If you touch that stove, it's going to be hot," is information and encourages awareness, rather than, "Don't touch it." My kids would feel the heat of the stove and would know not to touch it. There is, of course, always one child who has to test everything, but most of the time, if you give kids information instead of rules, it's amazing what will happen.

Magic is "ask and receive".
It's very light

Allowance

by Denise Levin

What is allowance? Allowance is observing what is without judgment. It is having no point of view about anything. Everything is just an interesting point of view.

What does that look like in real life? When I divorced and moved out of our family home, my children Ashley and Cole chose to live with their dad. I had to give up my own point of view about what our post-divorce family would look like. I allowed my kids their choice and regarded their decisions as an interesting point of view.

When other people commented to me that it was "terrible and sad" that I was ending a marriage of over twenty years and when I perceived their judgments about my "leaving my children with their dad," I didn't resist and react or align and agree. I was aware that it was just their point of view. It wasn't right, wrong, good or bad; it was simply their point of view.

I care for my children and I choose to let them create their lives as they wish. As a very wise man said to me a few years ago, "The best thing you can do for anyone is to set them free. Setting them free means you stop trying to do for them and you allow them to be and to experience their life as they choose."

Six months after I moved into my own place, my daughter told her dad that she wanted to "try" living with Mom. She never went back to living with her dad.

Even your children's point of view is just an interesting point of view. Children will manipulate you to get what they want, and just like anyone else, they'll use judgment to control you. Have you noticed this? I've had my children say, "Mom your breath stinks." "Mom you're a loser." "Mom, you're an idiot." Do I judge them for it? No, I've done the very same thing to them and to others. Interesting point of view, is it not?

I've found that when I don't align or agree or resist or react to other people's points of view, I am no longer the effect of them or their judgments. When I do not fight them or put up barriers to what they're saying, it gives them no place to go and nothing to battle against and (surprise!) they run out of steam.

Last year one of my children was really upset with me and spent several days being very unpleasant to me. I chose to think, "Interesting point of view that my child is choosing this," and within a few days I heard, "Mom I've been trying to make you miserable but I'm only making myself miserable. I'm going to stop it now."

Funny, isn't it how a little bit of consciousness leads to more consciousness and shifts everyone's reality?

When you're in allowance,
everything becomes
an interesting point of view.

You do not accept it;
you do not resist it.

It just is.

Get Your Pajamas on So We Can Read a Book

by Gary Douglas

If you truly desire to create and enjoy the possibility of conscious parenting, there is no room for limiting yourself with form, structure and significance by setting rules for your kids.

When my kids were little and I wanted them to go to bed, I'd say, "Go get your pajamas on so we can read a book." They would get their pajamas on, we'd read a book and they'd be asleep in half an hour

One night I said to my son, "It's time to go to bed." He said, "I don't want to go to bed." I said, "Well I'm going to bed, so when you're ready, turn off the light and put yourself to bed."

I went in my bedroom, turned off the lights, got into bed and pretended I was asleep. About half an hour later, my son looked around and saw that nobody was there. He turned off the television, turned off the lights, got into bed and went to sleep. That was the last time he ever stayed up later than I did. Objecting to going to bed wasn't nearly as much fun when there was nobody to object to.

If you have kids who refuse to go to bed, you have to be willing to go to bed and let them be responsible for turning off the lights and putting themselves to bed. Let them be aware of what occurs when they stay up until two in the morning. When you wake them up at 7:00 a.m. for school, and they're tired, you can say, "Sorry. You're the one who stayed up last night."

It's a little like touching a hot stove. Sometimes you have to do it once to have the awareness that you don't want to do it again.

> *The joy of being alive is the willingness to be the expansive infinite being you truly are.*

What Else Is possible? Let's play!

by Claudia Cano

One day when my son Alejandro was eighteen months old, I was doing laundry, and Alex was sitting in the middle of his room surrounded by his toys. He asked if I could play with him.

I said, "Sure honey, as soon as I take these clothes to the laundry room," which was on the third floor.

I started climbing the stairs with the laundry basket, which was so huge it could hardly fit through the staircase. When I got to the third floor, I perceived that someone was staring at me.

I turned my head towards the terrace and there, sitting in the middle of the terrace surrounded by his toys, in the same position he had been sitting in his room, was Alejandro. He was looking at me with a huge question mark in his face. "What took you so long?" he asked.

I was speechless. He said, "Well, let's play!" The question, "How did you get here?" popped into my mind. I didn't ask it out loud. He said, "I just did! Are we going to play now?"

I laughed and asked, "What else is possible?"

Alex said, "Yes, mom, what else is possible? Let's play!"

> ### *The magic begins when you're willing to perceive what is possible.*

Do I Control Them or Do I Let Them Go Wild?

by Gary Douglas

When I was growing up, I did babysitting to earn money. I worked for two distinct kinds of parents. The first kind were those who had long lists of rules that their kids had to follow. These parents weren't big on communicating with their kids. They focused on telling their kids what they could not do. The second kind of parents had a much more communicative inter-relationship with their kids. The kids of the first kind of parents, the rule makers, were the most insane to deal with. The kids of the more communicative parents were far easier to get along with and they turned out to be better people.

There are also parents who could be called "permissive." They allow their kids to do whatever they want to do, without ever communicating or sharing with them an awareness of what can occur. These parents follow behind their kids, picking up their messes and taking care of them. They don't want to have confrontations with their children. This is not what I am referring to when I talk about communicative parents.

Communicative parents communicate with their kids all the time. They are present with their kids energetically and they acknowledge who their kids are. They're not saying, "Oh, go do what you want in the world. I'm not going to be here when you get back."

It's more like, "How did your day go today? What did you learn? What is showing up?" The parents are communicating with the kids; they're not trying to control them. Communication is the key.

However, there are some places where a little control is helpful. When my kids were really little, I'd say, "Okay, let's clean up your room," and they would say, "No. I don't want to!"

I would take their little hands and together we would pick up each thing and put it in the toy box. I wouldn't clean their room up for them. I had them do it. This was more work than doing it myself, but after a short period of time, when I would say, "It's time to clean up your room now," they would clean it up. They learned that they could clean up their room when they were asked to.

I am talking about becoming aware of what is required of you to be with your children in each moment. It is not about control or no control. Many parents often want to do either/or. "Do I control them or do I let them go wild?" Neither. Parenting is not an either/or proposition. That, once again, is looking for an answer to for everything. It is wanting to get the answer right so that everything is taken care of forever and you don't have to be aware anymore. True parenting—conscious parenting—involves awareness. It's not about getting one answer and one rule and then enforcing it forever. It's about being aware of where your children are all the time, how they're functioning and what's going on.

> ***What would it take for you to perceive the possibilities, not the limitations?***

My Cool Three-Year-Old Friend

by Simone Milasas

I never thought I would have such a cool friend that was three years old. I did not think it was going to be like this. When my brother and sister-in-law had a baby, I never thought that I would be so grateful for my niece. Yes, I'd rather hang out with her than most adults! How does it get any better than this? I am also incredibly grateful that she is not mine. Having children has never been something I have desired—ever. So how did I get so lucky that she chose to be my niece! And I know she did.

So how amazing and aware is my niece Ellen? Very. For starters, she managed at just ten months old to get me to move in with her. I had not lived with my brother for twelve years, and when he and his wife and their one aware child moved to a small property, Auntie Simone also moved in. I was not aware at first that it was Ellen's idea. It just happened. So I got to spend about two years living with them and becoming Auntie Simone. Ellen and I now have an extraordinary relationship. She has an amazing ability to communicate with me no matter where we are.

A couple of days before Christmas, I was at a supermarket with my mother and Ellen. The place was jammed with people and everyone was frantic about getting their shopping done. Desiring to get out of the supermarket as quickly as we went in, I thought I'd run ahead and grab the few items we required, while my mother had Ellen in the shopping cart. When I had gathered the things we needed, I asked, energetically, "Okay Ellen, show me where you are." I moved from aisle to aisle, asking, "This one?" and I'd perceive the energy of "yes" or "no." I found them within minutes.

The amusing thing was, my mother said that just before I found them, Ellen had started yelling (and she doesn't have a quiet voice), "Auntie Simone! Auntie Simone!" Did she hear my energetic question, "Where are you?" Absolutely.

> ***The joy of being alive is an awareness of all things. It is the oneness that we all are.***

The Single Mother of a Teenage Daughter

by Margaret Braunack

Being the single parent of a teenage daughter has been one of the greatest challenges I have met in my life.

My daughter's dad walked out on us when she was three years old. Her brother, who was two years older, was particularly angry after the marriage breakup, and my daughter seemed to be on the receiving end of his anger. She coped with me working four jobs while studying, and then what spare time I had, she had to share with her brother.

All was well as far as I was willing to see, until the end of her first year in high school, when she started to fight with me constantly.

Her choice of friends left me cold and she started drinking alcohol on weekends with her school friends. She also started smoking. It seemed that I had lost my beautiful daughter.

I was at a loss. I didn't know how we could regain what we once had.

We could not so much as look at each other without it turning into an argument. My despair became so great that I even considered the option of sending her to live with her father, which was for me, was real desperation.

It eventually became apparent to me that the constant fighting was not working for either of us. The separation it was causing was unbearable for us both.

Luckily I had been reading lots of personal development books and had started to attend courses, which opened me up to look at me. I became aware that it was I who had to change. I had to change before she could see new possibilities.

Indeed, I changed and our life together changed, and miracles started to show up. I started to listen to her, and not just with my ears. I started to perceive her energy, before she even opened her mouth. I connected with her like I never had before. I always knew what was going on for her.

I made time for us to play together. Sometimes we took our Golden Retriever to the beach for a run. Sometimes I would pick her up after school and we would head to the local coffee shop for some decadent sweets. Sometimes we would go to the movies or go out for ice cream before dinner. Sometimes she would come and sit on the edge of the bathtub and chat with me while I was relaxing in a bubble bath.

The more I was willing to be me, the more my daughter changed. The more that I let go of my judgment, the more she let go of hers. The more I was willing to choose for me, the more she could see that it was okay for her.

> *Magic is not about using force and effort as a way of making things occur in your life.*

Who's Dating My Dad?

by Joy Voeth

Until recently I was allergic to children. Even when I was a child, I did not feel comfortable around other children. Later in life, I thought that if I had a child of my own, I would probably forget to feed it or leave it behind somewhere. I say this tongue-in-cheek, of course, but there is an element of truth in it. When faced with children, I had no idea what to do. Yet, once I became an adult, children seemed drawn to me. Perhaps I was different from the other adults around them.

At one point in my life, I had a relationship with a man who had a seventeen-year-old daughter, J. She had "emo" down to a fine science. "Emo" is a more emotional offshoot of punk rock and the culture that goes along with it. J wore black nail polish, black eyeliner and black clothes all the time. She smoked at least one pack of cigarettes a day. She was trauma and drama looking for a place to happen.

Underneath all the black, J was an expressive writer, a fiercely caring friend, a loving daughter, and a highly perceptive, complicated, young woman. I could see that, but could she?

When I began dating her father, she gave me the "I'm the only woman in my dad's life" routine. She would say anything she could to shock me or scare me away. She could be a real *%@# sometimes!

I did not set out to create a friendship or a "step-mother-daughter" relationship with J. I was willing to simply be around her, to continue to create my life, to listen, to ask questions, and not align and agree or resist and react to her drama. I soon saw that when I was in allowance of her, which did not mean being a doormat to her teenage tirades, she would run out of steam quite quickly.

One day, J came out and told me that she was a lesbian, well, bisexual actually, but that she really preferred women. Men were just her playthings. She told me all kinds of stories about how outrageous she had been and seemed disappointed that none of this had any effect on me. Every lightening bolt she threw my way, just blew through me, as an interesting point of view. I was not the least bit shocked. I had no judgment of her, her points of view or her choices.

That conversation began to open a door. I continued to ask her questions about her life. Was it working for her? What would she like to create differently? Would her life look different if she did not make other people's points of view solid and real? I asked all these questions, not from a place of trying to fix her or correct her, but with simple interest and curiosity. I just asked questions and followed the energy. I would wait for an opening when I could say the one thing she didn't want to hear that might create a question in her universe.

She began to seek me out to share the happenings of her dramatic life, and very slowly, things started to change. J began to trust me. She was still sullen most of the time, but she began to laugh occasionally. She would expose her father's secrets (no manipulation there, I'm sure) and would still try to dominate, manipulate, and control me whenever she had the chance—but that's part of a teenager's job.

What was more important to me is that she started to show more of the kindness and caring that she truly is. A delicate relationship began to blossom between us.

> ***What would it take to receive
> everything, with no judgment?***

Who Does This Belong To?

by Dr. Dain Heer

Recently, my sister asked me if I would speak with my seven-year-old nephew, Steven. Steven's baby sister, Talia, had just come home from the hospital, and when Steven held his little sister, he became afraid he would hurt her. My sister said Steven was very specific. He didn't say he was afraid he'd *drop* Talia. He said he was afraid he'd *hurt* her.

Steven became agitated each time he held Talia or was in close proximity to her. Just before my sister called me, Steven's father had asked Steven to bring him a knife from the kitchen so he could cut something in the bedroom. In order to get the knife from the kitchen to the bedroom, Steven had to pass by his baby sister, who was sleeping in her crib.

Steven got the knife from the kitchen and was taking it to his dad but he wasn't able to walk past Talia. He stopped before he reached her and began to cry. He finally dropped the knife and find his Mom.

When I spoke with Steven, I first asked him to describe what was going on for him. He told me that sometimes he felt "crazy" around Talia, especially when he was alone with her. He said that at times he felt like he wanted to kill himself and her.

I asked him, "Are these thoughts and feelings yours, or is it possible you are picking them up from someone else?" Steven asked, "What do you mean? I feel them!"

I explained to him there was a difference between feeling something and perceiving it. I said, "When you *feel* something, it's like it comes from you. You are the one with the point of view, the thought or the feeling. When you *perceive* something, you're picking it up from the people around you."

To give him clarity, I asked him if he ever knew when people were angry, sad or unhappy even without talking to them. Steven said, "Of course, Uncle Dain! Everybody knows that!" To which I replied, "Are you feeling their anger or perceiving it?"

He immediately understood that he was *perceiving* their anger. He understood that *perceiving* the anger meant that he was *aware* of it, and he saw that it was different from feeling or experiencing his own anger.

Steven began to see that *feeling* thoughts and emotions meant that they were his, but *perceiving* them simply meant he was aware of them. This meant he didn't have to "own" thoughts, feelings and emotions that weren't his. He could just let them go, since they didn't have anything to do with him in the first place.

I asked him to look at the feelings of wanting to harm his little sister and to ask the energy of the feelings and thoughts, "Who does this belong to?"

He did this and said that the feelings "lightened up" a bit. In other words, they became a little bit less intense. But they didn't go away completely, so I knew there was more work to be done.

My next question to him was even stranger, but as most children do, he took it completely in stride and even surprised me with his answer. I asked him if he was having the thoughts about hurting his sister, or if it was possible that he was hearing them, as if someone was talking to him.

He asked what I meant. I explained that sometimes entities (some people call them by other names such as ghosts or spirits) attach themselves to us and talk to us or tell us to do things, which can be very troublesome.

I said that there are usually lots of them in hospitals, such as the one in which his sister was born. I asked him if he ever heard entities talking to him. He said that he didn't hear them exactly but that he could feel them.

He asked me if what I was talking about was like when Spider Man is crawling on a building; he might not see what's coming after him but he knows it's there nonetheless. Steven called this "Spider-sense." He said that's the way it was with him and the ghosts I had just told him about. He knew they were there and could feel them, but he had never told anyone about it.

I let him know that the awareness he was having was actually a good thing, not a bad thing. I said him, "That's right! You have Spider-sense just like Spider Man."

He was very proud and happy about this, as any seven year old would be. I'm thirty-seven and I'd be proud too, if someone acknowledged my Spider-sense.

Once I acknowledged his newfound ability, Steven's demeanor and energy changed so much I could perceive it over the phone. I asked him if the feelings of wanting to kill his sister might be created by entities.

He initially said, "I don't know," so I just suggested he ask that question out loud. I heard him say, "Are any of these feelings of wanting to hurt my sister from entities?" He said the answer was "yes." So, I asked him if he would be willing to let the entities go.

He was willing. I did a very quick process to release the entities, a process that any Access facilitator can do. It took about 35 seconds. Then I asked Steven how he felt.

He said he felt "less heavy." I asked him when he first noticed the "heaviness," as he described it. He said he could remember it as far back as the hospital when he first walked into the room after Talia's birth, but that he couldn't remember if it was there before that or not. Apparently, an entity attached to Steven at the hospital when he went to visit his mom and Talia, and apparently it had been suicidal. This was why Steven wanted to kill himself and his sister.

After this clearing, I suggested he stay on the phone with me and have his Mom leave him alone with his baby sister, so he could be in the situation that had created difficulty for him. His mom left him alone in the room with Talia and I asked him how he felt.

He said he didn't feel "crazy" anymore, and he didn't have the "weird feeling like panic" any longer either. He said he felt fine around his sister and had no fear of harming her any longer. This took about 10 minutes to accomplish. A job well done . . . almost!

A few days later, I called to check up on Steven. My sister informed me that Steven's teacher had called her. Steven had been telling friends at school that he used to want to kill his baby sister, but he didn't anymore because he realized that it wasn't him; it was the "voices in his head." Oy!

So I suggest letting your kids know that there are some places in which they can speak about this "weird" stuff with ease and abandon, and there are some places where it doesn't work so well.

Unfortunately, school is not a place to talk about things like getting over the voices in your head. Simply ask kids to be in their awareness regarding when to talk about such things.

As this story about Steven shows, when kids experience uncomfortable thoughts, feelings and emotions, they might be picking up on the emotions of the people around them. It's often very helpful to ask them, "Who does this belong to?" If the thought, feeling or emotion, lightens up at all (becomes less intense), it's not theirs. Ask them to return it to sender.

Our kids are not only aware; they are psychic. They pick up on many things most of us adults gave up on long ago. They pick up on the thoughts, feelings, and emotions of others all the time. If we're not aware of this, we may attribute thoughts, feelings, and emotions to our kids that don't even belong to them.

The second bit of awareness to be had from this story is that kids are often aware of entities. They perceive entities as voices in their heads or as an impulse to do something. An Access facilitator can show you and your child how handle this in a very short amount of time, and before you know it, you'll be clearing entities like a champ. If you have any questions about how to do the entity clearing, ask your child. Once they learn how to do it, they remember it. Maybe it's that Spider-sense they're still willing to have that we gave up on a long time ago. They're not nearly as dense as we adults.

Lastly, when in doubt about anything with your kids, ask them questions. If you do so, you will help them to access their own knowing—their own Spider-sense. That's a gift they can use for the rest of their life.

> ***Consciousness includes everything and judges nothing.***

Is This Yours Or Are You Buying Other People's Stuff?

by Claudia Cano

We were at the park playing with the scooter. Alex, now seven, wanted to get home, but my mom wanted him to be active for a while longer so she "challenged" him to ride the scooter as fast as he could. He was reluctant, but she promised him this would be the last round. So he did. He flew like a rocket. Two seconds later I heard him screaming and crying. I ran to him. He was holding his right arm with his left hand. He looked me in the eyes and said, "My bone is broken."

It was true; I could see a curve in his forearm. Putting my hands on both sides of this arm, I began doing a hands-on Access process called MTVSS. As we were walking towards the car, Alex stopped crying and asked, "How does it get any better than this?" and "What else is possible?"

When we arrived at the emergency room, Alex was "fine," but as soon as people started regarding him with expressions on their faces that said, "That looks painful" and "Poor kid," Alex started crying and "hurting" again. I asked him, "Is this yours or are you buying other people's stuff?" He said, "Not mine! Return to sender."

When we got to the exam room, the doctor looked at him and said, "It's broken and judging by the bend in it, I think it will need traction or an operation." Alex's expression started to change, and I whispered to him, "That's an interesting point of view, isn't it?" He smiled at me.

I asked Alex to ask his body to heal and align his bone. I suggested that maybe his body would tell him what he could do to help it.

He then he told me keep holding my hands on his arm and to press a little harder instead of lightly touching it. I continued to hold his arm between my hands while we waited for them to take him to x-ray.

The doctor prescribed morphine in Alex's I.V. to ease the pain that he didn't have. He didn't bother to ask; he just assumed Alex was in pain, after all, he had a broken forearm! Alex started feeling dizzy as soon as the drug flowed into his body, so I asked him, "Could you ask your body to do something about it?"

He said, "Yes," and as soon as he asked, "Body could you do something to get rid of this?" the nausea and the dizziness disappeared. They then arrived to take him for an x-ray.

As we walked down the hall, I kept my hands on his arm, still applying a bit of pressure where the break was.

After the doctor viewed the x-rays, he told us that two bones in Alex's arm were fractured and one was slightly out of place, but not as much as he had thought, and that Alex wouldn't need anything more than a cast. He placed a cast on Alex's arm and gave us a prescription for Tylenol with codeine.

When we got to the car, I asked Alex, "What do you and your body know? Is it necessary to get the Tylenol with Codeine or should we just get Tylenol?" He said, "Nothing." …. I double-checked, "Nothing?" "Yes, nothing!" "Okay!"

When we got home, Alex had a wonderful sleep while I kept running Access energy processes on his bones. He didn't complain about anything that remotely felt like "pain." Actually, he didn't complain about anything at all.

> *The greatest power is the ability to change, transform and choose.*

You Have to Honor Your Kids' Point of View

by Gary Douglas

Most parents have misidentified and misapplied what caring means. For me, true caring is about acknowledging the infinite choice that kids have. True caring is being willing to allow kids to make choices even if you think those choices might hurt them. Most parents think caring means something like, "I love my kids and I care about them, so I will have them do everything I've decided is best for them. I have to tell them what to do because they are too young to make decisions for themselves."

At one point when Grace was four years old, she decided she didn't want to go out with us. She wanted to stay home by herself. I said, "Okay dear, if you want to stay by yourself, fine. I'll let you stay by yourself. We'll see you later. Goodbye." I was, of course, thinking that would be enough to scare her out of wanting to be home alone. But she wasn't scared. So we left the house.

Well, I didn't really leave. I stood outside the house and watched Grace through the window for about twenty minutes. She never got upset. After a while, I got out my cell phone and called the house. Luckily we had answering machine in those days and she heard me say, "Grace, how are you doing? Is everything okay?" .... "Boo-hoo!" She started crying.

I said, "We just thought maybe you might want to come with us. Do you want to come with us?" "Yes! I want to come with you now!" "Okay good, come with us."

You have to be willing to do those kinds of things with your kids. Take time to let them have their point of view and decide whether they want to change it or not. That's the most important thing you can give them—the understanding that their point of view is okay.

Most parents try to force their kids into doing what they want them to do: "You're going with us, young lady." That doesn't honor that they have a point of view. You have to understand that your kids have a point of view and honor it. You can do this by asking them what they desire and honoring their request.

Choice is your creation!

Why Would I Impose My Point of View on My Children?

by Gary Douglas

When my son was two, I bought him a tent. He wanted to sleep in his tent by himself outdoors. So I put the tent up right outside my bedroom window. When he was ready to go to bed, I said, "Here's your flashlight. Is your sleeping bag ready?" "Yup. It's ready, Dad." ... "Okay, good night." "Good night, Dad," he said in a deep voice and went to bed.

He stayed out there all night many nights, and if he woke up, I would go out there, pick him up, and bring him inside. But for the most part, he slept through the night because he was doing what he wanted to do.

Allowing your kids to function from their choices and decisions makes everything better in their lives, because they begin to rely more and more on themselves and their confidence grows. They begin to see themselves as valuable. They see that their point of view is not wrong.

I had friends who said, "Oh my God! That's too young! How could you let a two year old sleep outside by himself?"

I said, "The window is open. I can see the tent. I'm right here and I don't sleep very soundly. The TV is on and he can hear it until 11 o'clock, so if he really wants to come in, he can."

He even made me turn off the porch light because it was too much light shining in his tent, which was very funny. My kids are very independent because I didn't try to impose my point of view on them.

> ***When you are in allowance,***
> ***everything is an***
> ***interesting point of view.***

Parenting as an Interesting Point of View

by Curry Glassell

What does the phrase "parenting as an interesting point of view" mean? Well, what it means to me is that I speak with my boys in a different manner than most of the parents I observe. When I speak with my sons about difficult subjects, I do not attempt to impose my point of view on them. Instead, I ask them questions to get them to look at what *their* point of view is and whether that viewpoint is working for them and creating joy and ease.

One afternoon, my youngest son Sam, was acting very demanding, so I asked him if he would like to go to Starbucks and get a Frappuccino. He really likes them and so do I.

So off we went to get our drinks. We ordered and stepped outside to sit down. He was acting very high-strung and irritated and so I began to ask him questions about his schoolmates.

Since he had recently returned from a visit with his father in Oklahoma, I asked if everything went okay there. The expression on his face and the energy within his body told me something had occurred at his father's that was bothering him. He began to interrogate me as to "why I had taken all of his father's money and left him penniless and stranded."

"Well ..." I slowly began to respond and keeping my best poker face, I asked Sam what gave him the idea that I had done such a thing.

As he began to unravel the details of what his father had told him, I kept silent. I did not interrupt for 30 minutes while I watched my son suffer in his mind and body with the lie that he had bought as a truth from his father. Sam contorted himself as he attempted to fit this questionable idea into how he felt about his own mother with whom he was living and upon whom he was dependant for basically everything.

I continued to only ask questions and kept destroying and uncreating my own upset with his father for telling this outrageous lie to my son. "Why would you do that to daddy?" he asked.

Well, instead of denying I had done that, I instead asked, "Sam, does this story about what I did make you feel light?" "No," he said.

Then I asked him, " Do you perceive that this is what I did?" He looked at me and thought for a while, then shook himself and said, " Mommy, it does not feel like the truth to me."

I said, "Okay, lets look at all the pieces. What do you know about all the people involved in this story?" I worked with Sam, asking him questions about every detail of the story without intruding my opinion into the conversation. I simply allowed him to look at the energy of this story and know for himself.

All of a sudden he burst into tears and jumped onto my lap and said, "I am so sorry, Mommy. I really believed Daddy that you did this mean thing to him, but you didn't, did you?

Then I responded, "Yes Sam, my darling. You are correct. I did not do this thing to your dad."

What would it take to receive everything, with no judgment?

Allow Children to Choose What They Desire

by Simone Milasas

I have always asked Ellen, my niece, what her body desired to eat. She was not a big eater when she was a baby and there are so many confusions and fallacies about what a child should eat, so this seemed like the best way to make sure she got what she needed.

Ellen always knew what she wished to eat. Children are more aware of when their bodies are full and when they are hungry than most people are, and they choose to eat what their bodies desire.

Adults, however, make a lot of decisions about what to eat. They have a lot of ideas about what they *should* eat, but they never ask their bodies what their bodies desire. Ellen always tells me when she's had enough and she'll tell me what she desires. And guess what? It's not all chocolate and sweets.

Every time she goes to visit Grandpa, she asks him to cut up an apple and to eat it with her. She quite often chooses to eat the vegetables off her plate rather than anything else. And yes, she definitely attempts to con me into "Can I have a special treat?" Auntie Simone always says, "Of course you can." "Can I have Nutella twice in one day?" Auntie Simone always says, "Of course you can."

One day on the phone she told me she had been painting with feathers and "It was just as good as Nutella!" Interesting to see someone reference their life from a sweet tasting spread!

Ellen knows what to do. It's as if we haven't had to raise her; she knows what she wants, and she lets us know what it is. If we facilitate children's growth and allow them to choose what they desire, then I perceive we could have very aware, conscious children in our presence.

> *The ultimate power in this reality is the ability to change and to choose.*

Choice and Consciousness

by Dr. Dain Heer

One of the big things you can do with your kids to encourage their awareness is to ask them questions. What did you perceive here? What did you get out of that? Does this make you feel light or heavy? What did you perceive with this person?

When I was a child, my mom was very acknowledging of me as a being and didn't try to control me. It was very wise on her part, because I would have resisted control very dynamically. My dad and stepmother, on the other hand, did all the control they could, thinking that's what good parents did. Their attitude was, "We're going to show this boy how to live." In truth, they didn't have much to teach me because their lives were very small. It's interesting to have somebody who has a tiny life tell you that they know better than you how things are supposed to be done.

I also have a stepbrother and stepsister. My sister rebelled against my parents' control so hard that she almost killed herself with the alcohol and drugs that she was using and the abusive boyfriends that she was choosing. My half-brother, who is now twenty-something, is going through the police academy for the second time, and is actually graduating. He's been living at home his entire life. Until now, he hasn't been interested in holding down a job because his point of view has been that his mom should take care of him.

It took my sister until she was in her midtwenties to realize that it is up to her to create her life. The same has been true for my brother. He's not willing to implement it yet, but he's starting get the idea that it's up to him to create his life. So, I've seen first hand how my dad and stepmother's desire to raise great kids led them to try to control us. This was not an effective way of helping us to create our own lives.

In my experience, controlling kids doesn't promote their awareness—but asking them questions from the time they're smaller than a grain of rice is an important way of encouraging their awareness and teaching them that they are the ones who create what shows up in their lives.

Consciousness includes everything and judges nothing.

What a Gift for a Mother!

by Glenna Rice

Since I've been doing Access, my children very rarely get colds and if symptoms do show up, they usually go away quickly, sometimes immediately. At any rate, symptoms never last more than a day. I have not missed one day of work to stay home with a sick child in the past two years—and I have three children ages three, nine and thirteen. Before I had the tools of Access and was less willing to be aware, a sick child created great stress in my life. I'd have to miss work, arrange doctor visits and care for an unhappy, sick child.

Now, when one of my children shows up with symptoms, I ask, "What are you sick of?" and because they are aware, they know. They say things like, "I'm sick of homework," "I'm sick of my dad being angry," "I'm sick of you yelling at me" or "I'm sick of mean kids at school."

Once they uncreate and destroy their fixed points of view, their symptoms go away. The truth is, conscious, aware children do not want to be ill. When given the choice, they will create their symptoms away with ease. Now, when my kids feel bad, they usually tell me after they have cleared it on their own. They come to me and say, "Mom, guess what? I had a headache; it's gone now. I cleared it." What a gift for a mother! With the tools of Access, parenting gets easier and easier.

One night a few years ago, my two year old, Roisin, started coughing. It was a terrible cough and went on for a while. I was not able to help her change it. I called in my older children and asked them if there was anything they could see that would help Roisin. My middle daughter Saoirse immediately lay down with my youngest and asked, "Roisin are you a humanoid?" (A humanoid is someone who is always looking to expand, create change and make a better world.)

Roisin, who was crying, nodded her head yes. Saoirse asked, "Does a humanoid need to be sick?" Roisin shook her head no. And it was over. Roisin did not cough again than night. How does it get easier than that?

Learning to receive is the greatest thing you can do.

Parents and Their Tendency to Be Overly Caring

by Gary Douglas

I often watch mothers try to prove how much they care for their children, instead of actually caring about them. I think caring *about* your children is seeing them for who they are, acknowledging who they are, being grateful for who they are and not judging them for not being who you want them to be. Caring *for* your children is doing everything for them. It's trying to make sure they're safe, trying to make sure they get everything they should have, trying to make sure you give them more than you can possibly afford and all that.

Most parents have misidentified and misapplied caring as controlling everything in their children's lives so the kids never make a choice that "hurts" them. When I was a little kid, my mother used to change my clothes every time they got dirty. I hated having to change my clothes all the time, but my mother believed that I had to have clean, freshly washed and ironed clothes at all times. I learned to make mud pies with my hands out in front of me so I would not get dirty. As a result, I became a very tidy person. I can do very messy things without getting dirty.

The point here is that you want your children to know that you care about them and that they can create their life and take care of themselves.

I met a lady whose husband is an extreme sportsman. When their daughter was a year old, he had her standing on his hands balancing. When she was three years old, he showed her how to operate a jet ski. The mother cares about her child, but she also knows that her husband, who is extreme in everything he does, also cares about his child. So rather than getting upset, she asked him, "Can you show me how she does on the jet ski?"

Her husband showed her how he had taught their daughter to operate the jet ski. She knew how keep safe on it and how to jump on and off it on her own. That's caring about your child, but not being over-protective.

How many things have you done that didn't turn out well and you said, "Oh boy! I won't do that again!" What if someone had tried to keep you from having the experience because it might not work out well? Would that have been truly helpful to you?

You have to be willing to let your children have bad experiences. That is the hardest thing for parents to do. You can want your kids to be safe. You can want to protect your kids from having bad experiences, but you can't stop bad experiences from happening to your kids if they are not aware enough to keep bad things from happening to them.

That's the reason I let my kids have bad experiences when they were little. I figured if I let them have those experiences when they were little, they would make up their own mind that they didn't want to have those experiences any more.

Children are aware of energy. From the moment they come in, they function more from energy than from words. "I'm hungry" feels a certain way. "Mom and Dad are getting angry" feels a certain way. "Something's not right here" feels a certain way.

When you let kids have "bad" experiences, they learn about the energy that that precedes and accompanies a bad experience. They become aware and know, "Oh! When I've felt this way in the past, it was a bad experience. I'm going to choose something else."

When you help children develop their awareness of energy by allowing them to have experiences of all kinds, it helps to keep them safe for the rest of their lives.

All things are possible.

Helping Kids to Receive Everything Without Judgment

by Dr. Dain Heer

One of the ways parents can help kids to receive everything without judgment is by not judging their kids—or themselves—for anything. Kids are incredibly psychic and aware. They pick up every judgment we have of them and anything they're doing. They also pick up on the judgments we have of ourselves.

We've found that kids who grow up in households where there's lots of sadness end up believing it's *their* sadness, because the sadness is all around them all the time. If somebody who has sadness in their universe walks within five hundred yards of kids, they'll pick it up instantaneously and buy it as their own.

The same is true with judgment. If you function from a place of not judging yourself for anything you're doing (right or wrong), and not judging your kids, it creates a place for them to have space, and they realize they don't have to judge everything in the world, including themselves.

When Gary is with kids and they say, "I don't like this person," or "This person doesn't like kids," he asks, "Do you think he might have been a kid one day?" The kids say, "Yeah."

And Gary asks, "Do you think he was liked when he was a kid?" The kids say, "No."

Gary asks, "Do you think that could be why he does not like kids now?" "Oh, yeah!" "Okay."

The kids understand that the adult who can't receive them as children wasn't received as a child. When the kids say, "That person is judging me," Gary says, "Okay, so that person is judging you. Does that make you wrong? The kids answer, "No, it doesn't make me wrong." Then Gary asks, "And does it make her wrong?" And the kids respond, "Well why would she judge me?"

Gary explains, "In order to judge anything, you have to have been there and done it." The kids would say, "Oh, so she's accusing me of what she's done?"

Gary would reply, "Yeah, it's the only way it can be." This information about judgment gives them a sense of freedom. They understand that judgment is just judgment; it's not anything that's real.

Kids get it very quickly when you ask them these kinds of questions. When you ask, "Why does this person not like kids? Is it because he was not liked when he was a kid?" kids say, "Oh yeah."

It makes sense to them. They can see that's the case. They can then come out of judging themselves. They can also come out of judging the other person, because they see the whole picture. The clarity they get on it is quite extraordinary.

You have to give them tools to see where the other person is looking from, and why they might choose to do what they're doing. Once kids see this, they become willing to receive what's going on.

"This person doesn't like me." "Does she like herself?" "Oh ... no." "So how can she like anybody else if she doesn't like herself?"

> *Consciousness is only a matter of choice. If you choose to be conscious, then you can be.*

Being Aware Instead of Being Careful

by Gary Douglas

Many parents make the mistake of thinking it's their job to protect their children from things that might be dangerous. They try to keep them from doing anything that might hurt them. They try to keep them from doing things that are outside their own realm of reality. They want to make sure that nobody is going to run away with their children.

The problem with this approach is that it creates fear rather than awareness.

I didn't tell my kids not to talk to strangers. I said, "Be aware of who you're talking to." Half of the children who have been kidnapped, have been kidnapped by somebody they know. So, instead of saying, "Don't talk to strangers," it makes more sense to say, "Be aware, and if the energy doesn't feel right, get out of there. If doesn't feel right to talk to this person or if it feels yucky to you, run."

One of the greatest gifts you can give your children is an awareness of energy. They know when somebody doesn't feel right to them. You're actually keeping them much safer if you teach them to acknowledge their awareness of energies and people.

At one point my daughter Grace went to live in Mexico with her mother. One day when we were talking, Grace said, "Mom keeps telling me to be careful."

I said, "I don't know that being careful is what you want to be. You want to be aware because you don't understand every word of Spanish, but you definitely understand energy, and you know when something's not right. If something doesn't feel right, get the hell out of Dodge."

It is more important to be aware than it is to be careful. Being careful comes from the idea that everything is going to be bad and unpleasant. Being aware simply means you are attentive to the energy.

If you help your children to feel the energy of a situation and to take care of themselves by being aware, they will be able to stay out of trouble.

> *The joy of being alive is an awareness of all things. It is the oneness that we all are.*

No Mum, I Won't Be Careful, I'll be Aware

by Simone Milasas

People often tell kids to "be careful." What if being careful meant being paranoid that something bad was about to occur? What if we taught them to be aware instead of careful?

Even though the rest of the people around her are always warning my three-year-old niece to "be careful," I have been suggesting to her that she should "be aware."

She asked me, "What's aware?" My answer was, "You!"

One day she was walking down the stairs with a bunch of things in her hands, and her mum said, "Be careful, Ellen."

Ellen replied, "No, mum, I won't be careful, I'll be aware. I'll be aware of everything. Auntie Simone told me to be aware and Auntie Simone knows everything."

Fortunately, I have a great sister-in-law who thought it was funny and laughed.

> ***When you practice the art of
> choosing your life in
> ten second increments,
> you begin to create choice
> and the opportunity to
> receive infinite possibility.***

Daddy, I Want This Pendant

by Gary Douglas

One of the most important things parents can do for their kids is to encourage them to trust their awareness and perception.

When my kids were little, I used to take them out to garage sales. I would say, "Pick something here that is worth more than they're asking for it."

They would say, "Oh this," and I'd buy it. Later I would sell the item at a flea market for more than I paid for it, and I'd give the kids the money. They began to realize they could create money if they needed to, and they also started to see the value in things that other people didn't consider valuable. They started to look at the aesthetics of things.

Once when Grace was four or five, she went to a garage sale with me. She wanted to buy a statue of Kwan Yin. I asked how much it was and the guy said, "It's five dollars. It's Japanese."

As we walked away, Grace looked at me and said, "It's not Japanese, Daddy. It's Chinese." I asked, "How do you know that?" … She said, "I just know."

So I had it checked out. Sure enough, it was Chinese. Grace knew.

Another time we went to a garage sale and Grace said, "Daddy, I want this diamond pendant." I asked how much it was and the lady said, "A dollar."

I said, "Grace, you have enough junk jewelry, you don't need any more." She said, "Daddy, I want this pendant." I said, "Okay, fine, here's a dollar."

On the way home, she said, "I think the diamond is real. Look at the back." And so it was. It was clear from the way the pendant was made that the diamond was real. It turned out to be worth $425.

Grace has an ability to see what has value. I did everything I could to help my kids to accept what they knew to be true, and to be willing to receive that there was a different possibility in life. Our garage sale adventures were a very practical application of that.

> *The magic in your life is created from the true magic of you, which is the presence of you.*

The Favorite Aunt

by Margaret Braunack

My sixteen-year-old niece was just a few short weeks away from her Year Ten semi-formal dance. My sister is not one of the world's greatest shoppers, and her patience with her daughter at the time was not high. It was for these reasons that I was assigned the task of taking my niece shopping for the big occasion.

I found a time that worked for both my niece and me, and as my sister was avoiding the whole occasion, I was looking forward to making our shopping experience easy and joyful for both of us. My sister made it clear that the whole outfit, which included the dress, shoes, jewelry and handbag, was not to exceed $200.

Finally the shopping day arrived. I picked up my niece and on our drive into the city, I asked her what type of dress she would like. She said she would like a pink dress with shoestring straps that made her look slim. Just to make our task a little more difficult, my niece's body shape at the time was one that many styles didn't flatter.

After discussing the dress, I asked if it would be all right with her if we asked questions to allow everything to show up with ease. She said it would, so the first question I asked was, "Where is the best place for us to park for making our purchases with ease?" An awareness of a particular parking lot came in, so I headed there and easily found a parking place.

Then we asked what store would be the one to go to, to find the dress we were looking for. Within seconds, the name of a store came into my awareness, so we headed down the mall and into the dress section of that store. As we came off the escalator, my body turned me to the right, and I headed over to a rack of dresses. I immediately spotted a beautiful dusty pink dress with shoestring straps and beading around the neckline and hemline. I checked the size, and wondered what the possibilities would be of it fitting my niece.

We wandered around for a while, looking for other possibilities, and after finding a few others, we headed to the changing rooms. She tried the pink dress on first and it fit perfectly. She looked stunning. I knew that we had found the dress. She tried on the others just to make sure that she had the right choice, and after about ten minutes, we knew that it was time to make the purchase. At the cash register the sales assistant informed us that the dress had been reduced from $450 to $150. My response was "How does it get any better than this? What else is possible?"

I then asked which store would have shoes to match the dress. The name of a store came into my awareness, and we headed in that direction. Within a few minutes we had found a pair of shoes that were a perfect match for the dress, and they fit her like a glove. Once again, at the cash register, we were informed that the shoes had been reduced to $50 from $100. Again I heard myself asking, "How does it get any better than this?" and "What else is possible?"

Within minutes we had a purse and some beautiful jewelry to complement the outfit. The grand total for the outfit was $220, a mere $20 over budget, and the greatest gift of all was that we had purchased everything within one hour. We celebrated our purchases with a drink, and then headed home to share our shopping adventure with my niece's mother. She was pleased to hear we kept so close to budget, and delighted that the outfit looked stunning on my niece.

My niece is now willing to ask questions to allow new possibilities to show up in her life. Our shopping trip allowed her to see how easy life can be if you are willing to live in the question.

> *When you are in a place of no judgment, there is total allowance of all things.*

Talking to the Rain

by Virginia Mealing

It was my son Connor's seventh birthday and we were having some of his friends over for a party in the afternoon. The morning was rainy. When Peter, Connor's godfather, came over around midday and gave him a gift, he said to me, "Not a very good day for a birthday party. You're going to have six boys in the house making lots of noise."

I said I would ask the rain not to rain while the party was on. Peter made a face that said he thought I was cuckoo.

I went over to the kitchen window and told the rain that Connor was having a party from 1 p.m. to 4 p.m. and asked if it was possible not to rain during that time. I said, "Please let the sun shine during the party, and then after 4 p.m. it can rain as hard and as long as it wants to."

The boys started arriving a little before one o'clock and each parent was concerned about the pending rain. I told them it would be okay. Peter left to go home and phoned me about an hour later to ask how it was going with my request to the rain. He said it was pouring at his house, which is forty minutes away from ours. I said it was sunny at our house and that it could rain as much as it wanted over his way. He doubted me, so I took some photos of the boys playing in the garden.

Around 3 p.m., the clouds got dark and it looked as if they were ready to burst. I asked again, "One more hour, please. Our party ends at four."

It was a lovely party. The boys played and ate; then one by one went home. The last boy left at 4:10 p.m. and then down came the rain.

My three boys had heard me talking to the rain in the kitchen that day. Not long after that, we were at a BBQ and it looked like it was going to rain. The boys asked me to talk to the rain and ask it to wait for twenty minutes until the BBQ was over.

Instead of obliging them, I suggested to them that if I could do that, so could they.

> ***Would you be willing to function from total perceiving, knowing, being and receiving?***

Intertwining of Beingness

by Gary Douglas

Parents and kids often have very strong intertwining of beingness. By intertwining of beingness, I referring to a connection at an energetic level with another person. When you have an intertwining of beingness with your kids, you are aware of what they are unable to receive. Where they shut something out of their awareness, you get to receive it.

When Grace, my youngest daughter, would go out with her friends, every once in a while I would start to feel strange, and I would ask, "What's going on here?" I would call Grace and ask what was happening.

She would say something like, "My friend is drunk and getting into a bad situation." Grace was fine, but her friends weren't, and she was feeling what her friends were feeling and I got to feel what her friends were feeling, as well. Whenever this occurred, what she told me matched the energy I perceived and it put to rest my concern that she was having a problem. I simply wanted to make sure she was safe.

One of the greatest gifts I ever got from her was when she called me one night and said, "There are three guys over here drunk and four more on the way, and only three of us girls. This doesn't feel right. Will you call me and tell me I have to come home?"

I called her five minutes later and said, "Grace, I need you to come home now. I'm sorry to have to ask this of you, dear." ... She said, "Sure, Dad, if you need me, I'll be glad to come home," and she came home.

That's what you want as a parent—for your kids to be aware enough that if something feels funky, they won't to put themselves in danger.

One of the ways parents hinder their kids is by trying to get them to logic something through or to intellectualize it. They try to get their kids to think about the consequences of their actions. No! Don't try to get them to think about the consequences. Encourage them to be aware.

What I was doing with Grace was getting her to acknowledge that she was aware, so that she could recognize when the energy didn't feel right and get out of there. It was just a "feeling," an awareness that she had of the energy. She learned to trust those "feelings" and to know that because our beingness was intertwined, I'd be aware of what was going on, as well.

Because of the relationship I had developed with Grace her whole life long, when I perceived something weird in her universe, I could just call her and say, "I'm perceiving something weird," and she could tell me what was going on. She knows I won't judge her. If she asks me to pick her up, she knows I'll go and get her. I don't go into, "You're a bad kid and you shouldn't do this." You don't have to do any of that. Every kid is going to do something. They have to. It's part of growing up. You did it; we all did it. Why do we assume our kids won't?

> *The infinite oneness that we truly have and are is the source for everything that we would consider magic.*

It Is All Just Choice

by Gordon Issom

In February 2006, I received a call that my daughter Lou had just been released from the hospital, where she had been monitored for a few days. Thirty-two weeks into her pregnancy, she was displaying symptoms of high blood pressure. Not a desirable state. I immediately decided to go stay with her and her partner Damian in the wilds of northern Victoria, Australia in the gently named village of Bridgewater on Lodden.

Lou was pleased to see me, as she and Damian were busy trying to get their farmhouse finished in time for the baby. I could cook and be useful around the house. Her mother, who usually did these things, was in the UK seeing her own mother, so I was definitely an asset to the ménage.

On Sunday morning we were having a gentle walk before I was due in the kitchen to prepare a substantial roast lunch. Lou said she was a bit tired so we cut short our stroll and went home. Lou then declared she didn't feel well. Typically English, I offered to make tea. She was quite curt and said, "No, Dad, I *really* don't feel well." Damian was urgently summoned and the two immediately sped off to the local hospital, leaving me with strict instructions to feed the dogs and cats and get dinner ready.

I pottered around the house for an hour or two until the telephone rang to inform me that Lou had been given an emergency Caesarean section. The tiny baby girl and her daddy were in a neo-natal ambulance hotfooting it to Royal Children's Hospital in Melbourne, 100 kilometers away. Baby was too fragile to fly. She was ten weeks premature and weighed in at 1.2 kg (2.3 pounds). She was the size of my hand.

Lou had lost six liters of blood and was semi-comatose. I stayed with her in the local hospital where she was, as I could be useful there and she required some family support.

Michelle, our new baby girl, was technically DOA and she popped in and out of this reality three times on the trip to Melbourne. But the brilliant neo-natal staff at Royal Children's are a stubborn lot and Mishka, as we've taken to calling her, had things to do so, she stayed. The care of "preemies" is dependent on nursing, technology and will. The first two were in ample supply as Mishka was tubed all over the place and had her own constant nurse.

Mishka's placenta had been detached, and she had received very little oxygen for several hours before she was born. At birth, she was incapable of breathing without support and was having convulsions. When I first saw her, she was, to say the least, not attractive. She was a dark plum color. The people around her had somber faces and were talking in low voices about discontinuing life support treatment. I demanded we all wait until Lou was fit enough to travel and could at least see her daughter. Damian supported me and the treatment continued.

I had not yet been able to be alone with the baby and there were a couple of things I was determined to do. The first was to sing to her. (I love to sing early in the morning. I can warble like a lark. It has driven all my children mad for years, I am pleased to say.) I wanted to have a lullaby moment with my tiny little granddaughter. The second was to offer to her anything from myself that she desired. I also wanted to tell her that she didn't have to stay and fight if she didn't want to, but that she was loved and we would be happy to help her through her challenging beginnings. It was up to her. "Please stay, but you don't have to" was my message. She was the writer of her own script.

Well, Mishka decided to stay. First Lou came down to see her, and we managed to get Granny back from England at very short notice. Then the serious people were given permission to start taking away the life support systems. First the anticonvulsant medicine was stopped—but contrary to what everyone expected, Mishka didn't start having convulsions. Then the respirator was turned off—and to everyone's amazement, Mishka began to breathe on her own. The medical staff began to realize that this was someone "special." When she started at last to suck and gain weight, there was talk of going home.

Eventually everyone came home and I was able to be there to greet my lovely elfin grandchild, affectionately known as Millie Moo Face. She grew apace and is now over one year old. Miraculously, she has no damage to her system. She loves music and dance. We sing together, albeit in monotones, as she has yet to master the scale. My booming bass voice makes her little frame reverberate and she giggles.

She is the subject of the neo-natal unit's ongoing studies, as they rarely have such success. Her nurse has visited Mishka in her own home, a rare treat in that profession, and her doctor loves to trot her around the unit as an example of a miracle when she visits. It may well be a miracle, but it is Mishka's miracle, as she chose her dramatic entry, and she chose to stay.

I just ask, "How does it get any better than this?"

Live not in the effect of life,
but as the source of it.

Parenting From Awareness Is So Freeing

by Glenna Rice

Access kids create their lives from awareness, not fear. I am amazed over and over again when I observe my children in the world as they operate without fear.

My three year old taught herself how to swim by jumping into the deep end of the pool. With each jump, she would calculate the distance she could jump and swim back to the side. There was no fear, just joy that she could do it. I've also watched her ride an absolutely stunning white stallion with absolutely no fear in her universe, only intense joy.

She is able to play and learn this way in part because I do not have fear in my reality any more, so she does not pick that up and create it in her own. I would never limit her awareness by saying, "Be careful," "Don't," or "Watch out." I am able to perceive the energy, ask questions and be aware whether she is safe.

Parenting from awareness is so freeing compared to parenting from fear. I let my daughter create her life without the constant concern for her safety that most mothers have. Parenting from awareness allows me to experience motherhood as a joy rather than stress and hyper-vigilance.

The first time my nine year old was on a horse, she rode into a bee's nest. The horse started to buck and a handsome caballero pulled her off in a rescue right out of a romance novel. And she had no fear!

She said, "I was not sure what the horse was doing. I thought he might be eating grass because his head was going down."

When I complimented her on creating a fabulous rescue with the handsome caballero, she just smiled shyly. The next day, she got back up on a horse and rode as beautifully as the day before.

I watched my thirteen year old climb up in a tree and without any hesitation, jump twenty feet into the water below. I knew as well as he did that he was safe. I know that if I had had any fear in my universe, this would not have happened with the same ease and level of safety. When you parent from fear, you are not willing to be aware; you turn off your awareness and replace it with fear—and that is when kids get hurt.

Recently, there was a fire very near our house. We smelled smoke and saw flames across the road. My oldest son, who is thirteen, asked, "Should I call Gary?" I said, "Yes, good idea." Gary said, "Pack your stuff and get out."

Ten minutes later the firemen were evacuating our street. My son was as calm as I have ever seen him. He put the suitcases and computer in the car, walked up to me, put his hands on my shoulders and said, "Mom, the car is packed. It's okay, lets go." Our neighbors were frantic, but he was calm, cool and collected.

A minute later, as we drove away, with thirty-foot flames behind us, we asked our house to stay safe, along with everything in it. Our house listened and it's is still there.

> ***It is your definition of who you are***
> ***that defines the limitation***
> ***of your reality.***

Interesting Point of View
by Gary Douglas

To help your children learn to be in allowance and to
see things as an interesting point of view, you have to
function from "interesting point of view" yourself.
You can use "interesting point of view" as an
approach to every aspect of your life. Everything that
happens, everything that is said or done, is just a point
of view.

When my kids would fall down, I would never
run up to them and say, "Oh you're hurt!" or "What's
the matter with you?" I would see other parents
respond in that way, and soon after the fall, a bump or
a bruise would appear. They would create trauma and
drama around the things that happened to their kids.

When my kids fell down, I would say, "Did
you break the concrete?" They'd say, "No!" and run
away happy, without a bump or a bruise.

We also create a huge number of projections
about our kids' choices and what they're going to
mean. How many of the things your kids choose are
actually going to kill them? Not very many! Yet when
something doesn't go well for them, we act as if it's
going to kill them. No it's not; it's just going to give
them more awareness. If you can recognize that
probably less that a hundredth of a percent of the

choices they make could lead to death, maybe you could make the things they do a little less dire and significant.

If you start to encourage kids' awareness when they're young, they're just going to get more and more aware as they grow. They learn to trust their awareness and see it as something that's valid and real. It's something they can use to make their lives work well.

> ***When you are in a place of no judgment, you recognize that you are everything and you judge nothing, including yourself.***

Showing Your Kids the Good Life

by Gary Douglas

It's fun to let kids join you in appreciating the good things in life. When my kids were young, I had china demitasse cups for them. When I would serve tea, I would serve them a cup full of the regular black tea, but with cream and sugar, so it tasted good to them. They would have their demitasse cups of tea, and then they would go off and play.

They grew up using fine china as a normal thing. From an early age, they knew how to handle it. It wasn't something just the adults had access to. It was a part of their life too.

They also had little wine glasses. When we had dinner parties, they would have their juice in a little wine glass. And they used sterling silver utensils just like the adults.

If you're going to treat kids like they're one of you, teach them how to use china, glassware and silver, then they can handle them with ease when they're older.

Include them in special parties and mealtimes and allow them to have the same things you have. You've got to be willing to have things break, but this doesn't happen often. I find that ninety percent of the time, if something breaks, the kids are more devastated about it than we are. The next thing you know, they are handling things with more care than you are. A broken glass results in an increase in their awareness.

What if you celebrated your life every day?

Give Up Stuff That Is Not Working in Your Life

by Simone Phillips

Earlier this year, I was teaching German. I had a student in my class whom I had been teaching for two and a half years. She was in her third year of learning German as a foreign language at a high school in Queensland, Australia.

During our lessons I noticed that she was doing do a lot of negative self-talk, which she would often verbalize for everyone else to hear. It sounded something like this: "I can't do this work. It is too complicated. I have problems with my short term memory." And on it went. At times, when I asked her to complete tasks, she would use the negative self-talk as an excuse for not even attempting to do the class assignments.

By this time, I had learned to use many different Access tools. One day I noticed that she was voicing the usual objections and excuses and I called her over. We sat away from the other students who were working and I asked her whether she would like to give up all the ideas, negative self-talk and all other issues she had around learning a foreign language.

She said, "Huh?" So I asked again until I got a "Yes," and then we destroyed and uncreated the negative messages and beliefs connected with learning a foreign language.

What happened next was amazing. She started working and wrote a whole page in her German exercise book. She continued working every lesson, improved in her grammar and started participating and asking questions in class.

One willing teacher and a student who was willing to give up stuff that was not working ended up changing the dynamics of a whole class. How does it get any better than this?

You are an unlimited being.
You have unlimited possibilities.

Helping Kids to Be More Aware About Their Choices

by Gary Douglas

Parents often ask me, "What can parents do when their kids are about to make an anti-conscious choice such as drinking or doing drugs?

There are huge pressures on kids to take drugs, have sex and do what everybody else is doing, and they are probably going to experiment with these things at some point. Don't bury your head in the sand and say, "I told my children not to do that, so therefore they're not going to." That's crap. Your parents told you not to, and you still did it. Don't buy the lie that because you tell your children not to do something, they won't do it. This is a place where you, as a parent, have to be aware of the energy. You want to know that if your kids are doing something weird, it feels like this. If they're okay, it feels like that.

Do you remember when your kids were little, when it suddenly got too quiet in the house and you knew that something was going on? It's that same awareness. The same thing applies as kids get older. If it suddenly gets too quiet and you feel like you're being pulled into a vacuum, something's going on. They can be on the other side of the world and you can have that awareness that something is happening that shouldn't be happening.

Parents should never go into trauma and drama when their kids drink or do drugs or anything else. It should be, "Okay, how do we handle this?"

With my kids, I said, "Look, I know you're going to try drugs. I know you're going to try drinking. I know you're going to try everything, because that's what you do when you're a teenager.

"If you have a choice between drinking and drugs, I'd rather you choose to drink because it's still somewhat legal. I'd rather you not do drugs, because it opens the door to entities entering your body, which can be difficult to deal with later.

"If you're going to drink, be aware of who you're with. Don't cut off your awareness just because you're having a few drinks. You need to be even more aware than usual because you can get into a lot of trouble.

"You're probably going to do all of it. God knows, I did, so I don't expect you not to. I'm not going to tell you not to do this stuff, because that would be hypocritical on my part. I'm just going to tell you that doing those things weren't the best choices I made in my life. You might want to look at it and decide for yourself whether it's one of your best choices."

That's really all you can do for your kids. Give them the awareness of what their choices are and let them choose. Would you like them to be a certain way? Yes, of course. Will they be that way? Probably not. The question to ask is "What can we do as parents to help our kids be more aware about their choices?"

Are you willing to give up your fixed points of view of what it's got to be or what it has to look like?

Conscious Parents and Daycare

by Glenna Rice

A lot of mothers have viewpoints that keep them from inviting caring people to help them with the daily tasks of raising children.

A while ago, I sat in on a few mommy groups where the right and wrong and the good and bad of daycare, nannies and baby sitters were discussed at length. Mothers often have guilt and fear about leaving their children with someone else. Even in this era of the working mom, many parents experience difficulty with having other people care for their children. I have heard judgments like "Motherhood is the one job that you should never allocate to other people," or "Other people shouldn't be caring for your children."

The truth is there are many caring people with amazing talents and abilities who can often do a better job of taking care of kids than the kids' mothers can. Bringing these people into children's lives may be more caring than trying to do it alone.

For centuries it was the job of grandparents to help raise kids. Grandparents can give children caring and kindness that the parents are unable to offer because they are too busy "providing for the family." And if a grandparent is not available, a nanny or daycare provider can gift that same energy to your children. If you are trying to find caregivers from the point of view that only a mom can do the job, then that is what you will create. You may not even see the truly gifted caregivers who are around you because you will always be trying to prove your point of view, that mom does it best. This belief may also become your children's viewpoint.

When my youngest child was eighteen months old, I changed her daycare from a fabulous part-time nanny next door to a home daycare. Every day at drop off time, my daughter would cry and cling to me and then stop as soon as I drove away. This was so unlike her that I asked a friend for help. As we talked, I realized I was feeling guilty for changing her caregiver. The guilt was pretty hidden, but it was there. When I destroyed my guilt, the next day when I dropped my daughter off, she said, "Bye Mommy," and ran to the toys. She never cried at drop off again. When I changed me, my daughter's crying stopped. She actually liked daycare, but would cry because it went along with my point of view.

How do you find a great caregiver for your children? Ask questions. What will it take to create a caring provider who will work for me? Or ask the kids to have the amazing, cool daycare provider/babysitter they would like find them. If you ask, they will come.

I now receive so much joy from the help I get from babysitters, fabulous daycare providers and amazing grandparents because I have stopped judging myself as a mother and have become open to the unlimited possibilities.

Consciousness includes everything and judges nothing.

Dealing With Naughty Behavior

by Gary Douglas

What is naughty behavior? What is misbehavior?

Many parents define misbehavior as anything they don't like their kids doing. They send this message to their children: "You're misbehaving if you're doing anything other than what I've decided you should be doing."

I told my children, "If you do x, y or z, people are going to have serious judgments about you. They're not going to like having you around, and they're not going to want to have you in their home. So perhaps you should consider that this is not your best choice." Then, if they still misbehaved, I would send them to their room.

If they were out of control, I would say, "Go to your room until you're willing to be happy. You can come back when you're ready to be happy."

Another thing you can do is to give kids a name when they misbehave. When Grace was being obnoxious, I would call her "Gertie." "Oh we have Gertie visiting, do we? When is Grace going to return?"

Grace would say, "I hate that name! "Don't call me Gertie!" I'd reply, "Well then start acting like Grace, will you? Don't act like you're an obnoxious kid."

I had a friend whose little boy was named Sam. I said, "Give him a name when he's being naughty. What name would irritate the hell out of him?" She said, "Scruffy."

I suggested that every time Sam started acting obnoxious, that my friend call him Scruffy. Sam would start to act up, my friend would call him Scruffy, and Sam would say, "I hate it when you call me Scruffy! Don't do that!"

My friend would say, "Well then, start acting like Sam and stop acting like Scruffy." She would give him that choice and in a very short period of time, Sam would understand that he was misbehaving and he would choose not to misbehave.

Kids' behavior doesn't have anything to do with who they are. Their behavior is something they learn on television or from friends. They see other kids do that activity and get results with it. Be aware that they will spend hours practicing in front of the mirror to see which faces get the best results. I have caught all my kids at one time or another doing that one.

Give their behavior a name, because their behavior is not who they are. Then they can choose how to behave. You must be willing to let your children know what the rules are, without telling them that they are bad. If you tell kids they're bad, eventually they will come to the conclusion that they *are* bad. They become what you say they are.

Please recognize that some kids like being brats. I have dealt with several children that were not mine, that were hellions. Years ago, I had a friend whose child was so uncontrollable that people dreaded having her visit. That child would break everything in the house. The first time mother and child came over to my house I said to the kid, "Hey, let's go outside and look at the bunnies."

I took him outside and I said, "Look you little shit, you break any of my stuff and I'm going to break your arms and legs, and I don't care if your dad is a lawyer! I don't have enough money for him to take anything from me, anyway. You break my stuff, I'm breaking you. Got it?"

He looked at me and said, "Yes sir." He never broke anything at my house.

His mother said, "He never breaks anything when comes over here. He's so much better when he comes here than he is any place else in the world." I knew the boy was a little hellion, so I treated him the way he needed to be treated. I'm willing to do that with kids. If they're obnoxious and out of control, I tell them what the consequences of their behavior will be.

Being in allowance of somebody doesn't mean you have to be a doormat. You just have to be what is.

How Do You Deal With Your Kids' Sexual Energy?

by Gary Douglas

Kids come into life with incredible sexual energy and they are very "sexy" when they are young. When my son was young, he couldn't find enough ways to touch his penis. It was a handle he carried with him at all times. I had to tell him, "Son, when you're in public places, you need to not do that. When you're home, touch it all you want. Just know that some people will have judgments if you touch it when you're out in public. "

A lot of parents slap their children's hands when they touch their genitals. When they do that, they create the point of view that touching of that nature is a judge-able offense. What happens when they are suddenly old enough to have a relationship? Are they supposed to suddenly know it's okay to express their sexual energy?

You don't want kids to stop touching themselves, but you want them to be aware of what other people's judgments will be if they do it in inappropriate environments. Helping them understand this is probably the most important thing you can do to help your children create the relationship they will have with their own bodies.

If you don't function from a sense of judgment in your sexuality, sensuality and sexualness, it's likely that your kids won't function from judgment either.

I try to be very honest with my kids about what is possible and I try not to hide a lot.

We also need to educate our kids about how to choose their partners. There's not much information available about this. I've tried to teach my children to watch for a person who is sensual in what they do. When somebody sits on a velvet couch and starts to rub it, they are going to think that your body is nice to rub too. If they like to touch fur, if they like to caress the wine glass, they'll probably enjoy caressing you as well. If they treat things like they're pieces of wood and hammer them around, that's probably what they're going to do in bed as well. I tell my kids, "You want to be aware of the sensuality of people, because if they are sensual in the way they touch the things around them, chances are they will also be sensual with you."

I tell them that they can use this information to determine who they would like to have sex with. They can choose a truly sensual partner instead of a bad one that goes around saying, "Hey I'm such a stud. You want me." It gives them another option.

The point here is don't suppress your kids' sexuality. Help them to create a great relationship with their bodies and learn how to express their incredible sexual energy.

> ***Decisions and judgments always exclude anything that doesn't match them.***

"Special Talents" Kids?

by Gary Douglas and Dr. Dain Heer

Children who come into the world with Autism, ADD (Attention Deficit Disorder), ADHD (Attention Deficit Hyperactive Disorder) and OCD (Obsessive Compulsive Disorder) are often referred to as Special Needs Children. We would like to re-reference this point of view and call them Special Talents Children.

We have found that these kids are extraordinarily perceptive. They pick up whatever is going on around them. They are so aware that they oftentimes don't have the ability to discriminate between what is theirs—and what is not. Their ability to perceive is actually a skill and a talent, but they need some tools to learn how to live with it.

One of the important things we can do with all kids, but especially those that have OCD, is to teach them to discriminate between what emotions, feelings and thoughts are theirs and which are not.

If you ask children, "Are you perceiving this—or are you having this?" they will ask, "What is the difference?"

"Perceiving means that you are aware of something. Perceiving is stepping outside of something and looking at it. When you perceive something, it constantly changes from moment to

moment. It's like the wind. *Having* something means that it is in your body." When you explain the difference, almost every time kids will say, "Oh! I am perceiving it!"

This is an entirely new concept to them. People ask them questions like, "What is causing your feelings?" or "Why do you feel this way?" Nothing is causing their feelings and thoughts! They belong to other people. The kids are just picking them up. Teaching them the difference between perceiving feelings and having them sets them free.

Kids with Autism also pick up everything telepathically. Good luck giving them rules. Rules do not work. However, if you give them a whole picture of what you're going to do, where you're going that day and what you'd like them to do, they understand what's going to happen and what you want, and they calm down. Parents who have tried this way of communicating with their Autistic kids say things like, "This was the first time, that I can remember, that my child was calm all day long."

With any kid, when you're willing to communicate from the point of view that they have awareness and are aware of energy, they respond dynamically.

If you have children who have Autism, ADD, ADHD or OCD, give them tools that will help them learn to live with their abilities. Teach them the difference between *perceiving* emotions, feelings and thoughts and *having* them. Ask "Are you perceiving this—or are you having it? Does this belong to you—or are you picking it up?"

Consciousness is the awareness, the perception, the receiving and the being of all things without judgment.

Being a Valuable Product in the World

by Dr. Dain Heer

The other day, I was helping my mother with something she was going through and she said to me, "Don't you ever get tired of raising me?"

She is such a sweetheart. I said, "No, Mom! Since you've been doing Access, it's actually been fun!"

From the beginning of our relationship, my mom and I have been friends, and she gave me the great gift of acknowledging my awareness, even when I was a little kid.

At age five, I observed that she made coffee every morning, so I started making her coffee and bringing it to her. She would make my lunch and do everything she possibly could for me. I saw that one of the ways I could care for her and gift to her was by making her coffee in the morning. I was really excited when we got an automatic coffee maker and all I had to do was fill it up at night, hit the button in the morning and take her the coffee.

She always acknowledged my awareness and the gifts I gave her, and it allowed me to feel like I was an adult from the time I was very young. I wasn't operating from a place where I thought, "I've got to take care of the world and everyone in it." It was more like I had an awareness of myself as a valuable product in the world. This was something my mother gave me, and one of the ways she did it was by accepting my gifts.

Most parents don't acknowledge the awareness their kids have coming into this life and oftentimes they don't accept the gifts their kids offer them. This puts a stop on kids claiming the totality of their infinite capacity and awareness. As a result, the kids create limited possibilities for themselves.

Are there gifts your children offer you that you might not be receiving? Are there ways you could better acknowledge your children's awareness and their sense of being a valuable product in the world?

What kind of possibilities can you create today? What else is possible?

I Am No Longer at the Effect of My Children

by John S. Carter

As my use of Access tools has increased over the last year and a half, my relationship with my two adult children has been totally transformed. Most important for me, I am no longer at the effect of my children.

I'm much more willing to be me and not carry around an idea of what I think I need to be for them as a father. I share the tools of Access with them and they actually ask me questions now. I'm no longer in judgment of them. I don't require anything of them, and I especially don't think that they have to be or do anything in order for me to be happy. I'm open to the infinite possibilities of them creating their own lives.

Gone is the competition I've felt with their mother for their attention or approval. As a result, they seem much more open to the possibility of creating their own lives.

In a recent conversation with my daughter about an issue that was sticking her, I asked her, "How does it get better than this?"

She called a short while later to tell me that her life "had just gotten better." Something had shown up that she hadn't even considered. That's the power of a question: "How does it get any better than this?"

The greatest tool I've learned is to ask myself if I am being the five elements of intimacy with my children: honor, trust, gratitude, vulnerability and allowance. Am I honoring them? Do I trust them? Am I grateful for them? Am I being vulnerable with them? Am I in allowance of them and what they do?

Yes, I can say without hesitation that I have all of those today with my children. What else is possible?

Who are you today and what grand and glorious adventure are you going to have?

Conscious Kids
Live Not as the Effect of Life,
but as the Source of It

Stories by Kids

I Decided to Make Choices for Me

by Claire N (15) as told to Leena Dillingham

It was cold outside; I remember that. My mom was going to an Access energy workshop like she did all the time. She asked me if I wanted to go. She said it was weird, but I might like it.

Normally I would have said, "I don't want to go hang out with you somewhere where there is a bunch of old people. It's my winter break. No." But something made me say, "Yes."

I went, and I was like, "What is all this stuff? It's weird." But I felt so good afterwards. I felt so light and no one was judging me. The adults talked to me like I was a real person, which was a shock. I was like, "I want to do this over and over and over again."

I had been really depressed. I wanted to make changes in my life but I didn't know how. I kept choosing things that made life harder for me.

Once I started going to Access workshops, I stopped being so depressed, and I started making different choices. "You know what? I don't want to go smoke and drink with these people. I don't want to hang out with these people anymore." Within a couple weeks, I had completely changed all of my friends. I stopped doing all of the things that were bad for my body and me. I decided to make choices for me instead of choosing what everyone else was telling me I should choose.

> ### *Choose what you would like to have in your life.*

We Just Follow the Energy and Do Whatever Works

by Ashley L (16)

My mom is an amazing person. She lets me do whatever I want and doesn't try to control me the way other parents do. She was just commenting to me the other day about how independent I am.

Now at sixteen, I have my own car and I drive myself to my college. Mom acknowledges me as being independent because I go to school early in the morning to receive tutoring for my classes. She allows me to have a lot more freedom than other parents allow their children. Before Access she used to say, "Do your homework." I, being very defiant, would think in my head "No! I'm not doing my homework now. For every time she says, 'Do your homework,' I will put it off for another hour!"

But now that she has the Access tools, she uses questions to empower me! She asks, "Do you have homework to do?" It can be a little annoying, but it gives me an opportunity to look at the situation for myself and make my own choices. Rather than saying, "Put gas in your car!" she asks me, "Do you have enough gas in your car?"

Sometimes she says, "You have to clean up the kitchen by tomorrow or I'm throwing all your papers out." Then, at the least, I'll do it.

She doesn't make me do everything for myself. Nor does she do everything for me. We just follow the energy and do whatever works. If I have an appointment, she'll remind me of it because she's good at remembering things and otherwise I would forget. She doesn't make me do chores.

My mom allows me to have my choices in life. She doesn't control me or say things like, "This is the way it has to be." She lets me do whatever I want!

All she requires of me is that I be a kid. Amazing, truly amazing.

She used to say, "You're going to fail high school." I would get angry about this. Now when I make a choice she might not agree with, she says, "Well, interesting choice, Ashley."

My little brother does not attend the Access classes. My mother is in total allowance of that. She doesn't have a point of view that he should or should not be doing Access. She allows him to have his choice and she's fine with whatever he chooses. I've seen plenty of parents in Access who are not in allowance with their kids. They have decided their kid has to go to every Access class. I go to Access classes because I like them. It's my favorite thing in the world.

Recently, I had the choice of either going to my weekly riding lesson that my mom and I take together or staying at home and listening to a Christmas teleconference that was important to me. I chose to stay at home and my mom chose to go to the ranch for her lesson. I was happy. She was happy. When you're really communicating, you can honor someone else's choice and not align or agree with it or resist and react to it. Whatever my mom chooses is best for her. And whatever I choose is best for me. No judgment there.

Your imagination is a limitation, because imagination can only define what you already know.

Access
A World of Different Possibilities
by Brianna T (13)

Access isn't something to describe. It isn't something that you are forced into.
It doesn't make anything more valuable than yourself.
I am only 13 years old but I can relate to Access a lot.
Access is choice.
Access lets you choose and choose again.
I have always been raised to believe in Christ and that he is a wonderful God.
Access doesn't make you choose between God or Access, it just lets you have a world of different possibilities like when you are at school and you have to choose who you want to hang out with. Access gave me the possibility of being able to hang out with everyone and still choose for myself.
You should always be happy with what you are doing. You should choose complete happiness and bliss for yourself.

My Brother Pitched a Shut-Out Game!

by Ashley L (16)

One day after school, my brother and I were at home watching TV when my mom said, "I learned this new thing called Bars, which involves putting my hands on certain points on the head. Can I practice on you?" We both said, "Okay."

My twelve-year-old brother was lying on the couch and my mom started to touch points on his head. He said, "Wow! I can feel that! That feels good! Will you do that for me tomorrow?" My Mom said, "Sure, what's going on in your life tomorrow?"

My brother said he was the starting pitcher in his championship little league baseball game and he was nervous about it.

The next day my mom ran my brother's Bars for an hour and a half while he was lying on the couch watching TV. Two hours later, my brother pitched a shut-out game. A shut-out game is when nobody is able to get a hit off the pitcher, so nobody on the opposing team can score a run. It was the first time in my brother's life that he pitched a shut-out game.

My Dad, who is the baseball coach, doesn't believe in all of this "weird stuff," but he said to my mom, "Thanks, for doing that Denise. He was a different kid out there."

That's one of the nicest things my dad has said to my mom since they got divorced. To this day, my brother still asks my mom to run his Bars when he has a sports game or the night before a test or when he is sick.

Ask for the greatness of your life.

Okay Dad, You're Right

by Aubrey B (15) as told to Leena Dillingham

My dad is an angry person. He gets angry and he expresses his emotions. Now that I've learned so many Access tools, I can say, "Okay, Dad, you're right. I'm wrong. That's fine. I can deal with it. Bye-bye."

This has completely changed the dynamic, between my dad and me. We used to fight all the time, and now we have fun and joke and laugh and do stuff together. That was something that I never thought would be possible with him.

Magic is all around you;
it's something you create.

How Did I Get So Lucky?

by Alejandro Perez C (7)

Something my mom told me from Access that works for me is the thing about asking questions like "What are the infinite possibilities?" and "What else is possible?"

Once I asked, "What are the infinite possibilities of getting that toy?" and a few days later, my grandpa came to visit and he brought that toy for me. How did I get so lucky?

I asked that question once so I wouldn't have to go to school because I hadn't done my homework. I asked, "What are the infinite possibilities that I won't have to go to school tomorrow?" There was a snowstorm and they closed my school. I got to stay home and play in the snow. How does it get any better than that?

Asking questions also worked for me when we were playing bingo. I was losing and I asked, "What else is possible?" And I won.

Ask for the greatness of your life.

Now I Realize I Don't Have to Be Normal!

by Claire N (15) as told to Leena Dillingham

I was very depressed a year ago. I'd sleep all day, and I'd cry before I'd go to school and say, "I don't want to go. This is the last day, and then I'm quitting."

My mom was really expansive about it. She didn't try to force me into going. She was willing to consider a lot of different possibilities. She said, "What do you want to do? You can drop out if you want to. You can get a job. You can go to a different school."

Even though I hated school, I was stuck in "I'm going to stay in school. I'm going to stick it out," so I kept going. Towards the end of the year, I realized, "I can't do this!" and I switched to a different school.

At the time, Mom and I were fighting a lot because I felt, "I don't want to be here. I just want to die. That's all I want to do. I just want to curl up in a ball and not wake up."

Mom would say, "Okay, Claire, get up. Do your chores. Go to school. Go hang out with some friends, at least."

I was like, "No, I don't want to," then we'd fight about it. I'd scream, and run to my room and cry, and she'd scream and run to her room and cry. There was lots of crying.

Things changed after Access. If we have a problem or I don't want to do something, I'll ask, "What will it take to work this out?"

I can't even remember the last time we fought. We may disagree on something and we might pout and then we say, "Hmm," and we ask, "Well, what can we do to change this? Well, what works for you?"

We start asking questions, and things lighten up. Before you know it, we'll be laughing hysterically when a moment before, we were angry at each other. Within thirty seconds, we're saying, "Ha-ha, we're dumb!" We just make things work. My mom realizes that I'm a person. Actually, she's always realized that, but I'm really appreciating it now that she takes my opinion and my choices into account.

She says, "This is your life." I've really been trying to pick up on that lately and not give my life over to her.

Before Access I was searching and trying to find something that would make me fit in and be normal. Now I realize I don't have to be normal. Asking questions all the time, even random questions, like "What's your favorite flavor of ice cream?" lightens everything up. I've started using questions like, "What'll it take?"

I look at the decisions I make because I've made so many judgments and decisions and I see that I was creating a lot of junk for myself. I would decide things like, "She hates me. Well, I hate her, too." And then I'd wonder, "Why does she hate me?"

Once I started asking questions and looking at my decisions, I'd realize that the person I thought hated me didn't even know I was there! I started seeing how many crazy things I had created in my mind, not even in the world, just in my mind.

I'd say, "Oh. I just made a crazy decision. I'm going to uncreate and destroy that, and live in this space." It is really great.

> *You are creating your own life when you are willing to live in the present and you are not functioning from the past.*

Ask and You Shall Receive

by Claire N (15) as told to Leena Dillingham

My friend Aubrey and I wanted so badly to go to the Access class in Costa Rica, and we were asking, "What'll it take for us to get there?" We asked that together.

Then Gary announced to an Access Level Two and Three Class in Houston, "These girls want to go to Costa Rica and they're looking for sponsors. Their parents will pay for their airline tickets." A couple of people spoke up and said, "We'll pay." That's how I got there. I was in shock, "It can be this easy? Someone else will pay for me to go? You just ask?"

I am aware that I created this trip because I definitely asked a lot of questions like, "What would I have to do to get to Costa Rica?" and "What are the infinite possibilities?" As soon as I found out that the class was taking place there, I started asking, "What will it take? What will it take?" And it happened!

You are an unlimited being.
You have unlimited possibilities.

I'm No Longer Scared of Horses

by Sabrina F (7)

Once I was cantering on a horse down a hill with my mom and I got scared. I felt light-headed and started to cry. I thought I was going to faint.

My mom helped me uncreate and destroy everything that I was scared of and then she asked me, "Do you want to expand—or do you want to fall apart? What do you choose?"

I said, "I choose to expand." Mom told me how to pull energy from the earth up through the horse and out through the top of my head. I did this and I felt much better. I was relaxed and riding with the horse. It was amazing!

When you practice the art of choosing your life in ten second increments, you will begin to create choice and the opportunity to receive infinite possibility.

Ask Your Kids Questions

by Claire N (15) as told to Leena Dillingham

At my school, sometimes we have student-led parent meetings. After I led one of the meetings, parents came up to me and said, "That was amazing. You taught me so much. I never thought of things that way."

One lady asked me about her son, "My son hasn't been doing his homework, and he won't do his chores. He's feeling so depressed. What should I do?

I asked, "Well, have you asked him why he's not doing his chores and his homework, and why he's feeling depressed?" She said, "No, I didn't think of that."

Parents could help their kids so much if they would just ask questions.

Would you please claim and own the capacity to celebrate your life and make it a joyful experience every day, starting today?

What Would It Take for Me to Get an "A" on This Test?

by Ashley L (16)

I started Access when I was fourteen years old and in my freshman year of high school. I was unhappy with school even though I had a 3.8 grade point average in my first semester. I had to study for hours to achieve that result and I was constantly stressed about my grades. I thought that I had to get into an Ivy League school in order to have a successful life. I had tried reading several self-help books about how to reduce stress and get straight A's but I found that nothing helped.

Luckily, my mother started to run my Bars, even though I didn't know what it was, and that helped to alleviate my sleeping problems and my stress.

When it was time for my freshman year final exams, I was studying for hours every day. My mom ran my Bars every night and I was able to get A's and B's on all my finals. A few months later, when I was studying at home for my Japanese test, I was starting to get stressed out again. The teacher had said the exam was going to be very difficult, and I went into the trauma and drama of it. I called my mom, who was at an Access clearing night. She handed the phone over to Kacie, the facilitator, and Kacie talked with me for a few minutes. She asked me questions like "How many decisions have you made about this test?" and "How many lifetimes have you spoken Japanese?"

I didn't believe in past lifetimes, but I just went with it. Kacie then said a weird statement that I found out later was called a clearing statement. After that, I sat down and started studying again and it seemed much easier. I realized I didn't have to study nearly as much as I thought.

I walked into the test the next day feeling relaxed and had by far the best score in the class. I got an automatic A+ because our teacher grades on a curve.

> *It is your definition of who you are that defines the limitation of your reality.*

Helping Others
with Access Tools

by Ashley L (16)

In the last two and half years I've learned a lot of Access tools that I use in school. The most helpful things have been getting my Bars run and learning to ask questions. I ask questions like "What would it take for me to get an A on this test? What do I need to study?" It's amazing how easily the information I need comes to me. My studying time is dramatically reduced. I also destroy and uncreate my decisions, judgments and conclusions about things.

I felt like I had collected so many tools about studying that I wished I could share them with others, so I started tutoring people.

It's really been a lot of fun to work with people and tutor them in English or whatever subject they're having trouble with and to see the changes in them. Some of the people I've worked with have lived in the U.S. for twenty years but still didn't speak English well. They had tried classes, other tutors, and many other techniques but without much success. After a few sessions with me they started to have more confidence and their ability to speak changed dynamically.

As part of tutoring, I like to give kids fun questions they can use like "What would it take for me to read and write faster than I can possibly imagine?

> *The way to create everything you want is to be as wild and crazy and wacky as you truly are.*

I'm a Lot More Me

by Aubrey B (15) as told to Leena Dillingham

Before I started Access, I used to follow my friends around all the time, saying, "Yeah, yeah, uh huh," and many times my friends would say, "Okay Aubrey, I need a break from you because you're too clingy." And I was like, "Uh, okay."

Now I'm a lot more me, and a lot more okay being me. When I'm around my friends I actually show up and have a say in what we do.

I'm different in school too. I don't even call my teachers "my teachers" any more. They're more like friends that are older than me and have other smarts that they can share with me.

In the past, I remember going to lunch with my friends, and saying, "Oh, I hate this teacher, I hate that teacher. I hate this teacher more. Can you believe what she did?" Now I have much better relationships with teachers. I know each one of them. They help me.

Ask for the greatness of your life.

My Mom Was Choosing to Have Cancer in Her Body

by Kelsey T (11)

(Kelsey's original handwritten story is reproduced at the end of this section).

When I got introduced to Access, my mom was choosing to have cancer in her body. I wasn't taking care of my body. I was being there for my mom, cleaning up after her and taking care of my little brother and sister and not me. I was killing my body because of everything that was going on!

My sister Brianna went with my aunt to go do a yoga class! They asked me if I wanted to go, and I said, "No, I'm staying with my mom."

Then one day later, my sister calls me and says there is this amazing class called Access and said it was lots of fun and all these good things. I said, "I wanna go!" …. So they took me the next day.

This is the day I realized that my mom was choosing to be in the position she was in. So then I started taking care of my body. I used the tools that I learned, which were "How does it get any better than this?" "What would it take?" and "All of life comes to me with ease, joy and glory."

So when my mom would come and tell me how sick she was and when she would complain and tell me she needed more help around the house, I'm thinking in my head, "She's choosing this miserable life, and why should I? I don't want to kill my body because she's killing hers!"

So I stopped and I started choosing for me. It helped me a whole lot! Til this day, she knows we won't listen until she asks us a question instead of telling us!

Her body looks beautiful! So what would it take for everybody to choose for them and to destroy and uncreate their relationship with their parents?

I would like to thank Dain, Gary and my Aunt Sulema. I am so grateful for you guys. Thank you so much!

> ***When you are in a place of no judgment, you recognize that you are everything and you judge nothing, including yourself.***

8/1/07

Kelsey Access Paper

when I got introduced to access my mom was choo-sing to have cancer in her body. I wasnt taking care of my body. I was being there for my mom, cleaning up after her, and taking care of my little Brother+sister, and not me. I was killing my body Because of every thing that was going on!

My sister Brianna went with my aunt to go do a yoga class! ~~They asked~~ they asked me if I wanted to go I said no I'm steying with my mom. Then one day later my sister calls me and says that teir is this amazing class called Access and said it was lots of fun and all these good things, I said I wanna Go! So they took me the next day. This is the day I realized that my mom was Choos

to be in the position she was
in.

So then I started
taking care of my my body.
I said ~~the~~ the tools that
I learned wich were How does
it get any better than this,
what would it teke, And All
of Life comes to me with ease,
Joy, and Glory.

So when my mom ~~came~~ would
come and tell me how sick
she was and she would tell
me she needed more help around
the house. so while shes complaining
I'm thinking in my head "shes
choosing this miserable life so why
should I? I don't want to kill
my body because shes killing
hers! So I stopped and started
choosing for me! It helped
me a whole lot! Till this
day she know we won't listen

until she asks a ? instead
of telling us! ~~she looks so~~
HER body looks beautiful!
So what would it take for
everybody to choose for them
and to destroy and uncreate
their relationship with their
parents! I would like to the
this to Dain, Gary, and My
Aunt Sulema. I am so grate
full for u guys thanks
you so much!

           −Sincerely

            Kelsey

*Know you as the
greatness,
Perceive you as the
greatness,
Be you as the greatness
and
Receive you as the
greatness.*

Gary Douglas
Access Energy for Transformation

The Ten Commandments of Access

The Ten Commandments of Access are the key to get you out of the limitations of this reality and to create total freedom. If you will actually do these things, you will get free in every aspect of your life. They will set you free of the trauma and drama of this reality and assist you to create your life.

1. Ask "Would an infinite being truly choose this?"
2. Everything is just an interesting point of view.
3. Live in ten-second increments.
4. Live in the question (instead of the answer).
5. No form, no structure, no significance.
6. No judgment, no discrimination, no discernment.
7. No drugs of any kind.
8. No competition.
9. Do not listen to, tell or buy the story.
10. No exclusion.

More Information About The Ten Commandments of Access

Start with any one of the commandments and as you do it, it will begin to unlock the limitations in your life. Just pick one and start applying it.

If you undo the way you have been functioning from one limitation, all the others start to unravel as well.

When you have used these tools so much that they become part of you, you can function as the infinite being you truly are. When you add the five elements of conscious parenting to these ten commandments, you have the ability and awareness to create your life.

1. Ask "Would an infinite being truly choose this?"
If an infinite being wouldn't choose it, why are you? The only reason you are choosing something that an infinite being wouldn't choose is to make yourself finite and to create a disaster in your life. Isn't that cute? You didn't know you liked creating disaster did you? Oh yeah, you do, because the disaster is called your life.

2. Everything is just an interesting point of view.

Everything is just a point of view that is neither right nor wrong, good, nor bad. It is just a point of view. There is nothing to fight. I hear one thing and you hear something else. Does that make you right and me wrong? Does it make me right and you wrong? No! We just have different points of view. You cannot be in my body, hearing or seeing or being what I am, and I can't be in yours.

If you want to really get free, here is something you can do. For the next year, run "interesting point of view that I have this point of view" for every point of view you have. When you finish, you won't have a point of view about anything. "Interesting point of view I think this," creates total freedom and keeps you from getting stuck in any fixed point of view.

You can't have a fixed point of view when you are functioning from "interesting point of view." Everything is just a point of view you have taken for the moment; it doesn't mean anything. You can change it at any time.

3. Live in ten-second increments.

Do you live your life from "I have this to do, this to do and this to do so I can pay this, this and this, in order to do this, this and this"? That is called the obligatory version of life or the obligatory creation of reality.

If you have no point of view, you can choose to do anything. You do something for ten seconds, and if it doesn't work, you say, "You know what? I am not liking that. I'm going to choose something else." And then you do that for ten seconds. Then you make another choice.

Instead of living in ten-second increments, you keep trying to make yourself consistent. You think, "Well I chose this, therefore it is the right choice, therefore I am going to do it. I am going to do this, this and this because that is what I have chosen."

But life is not about choosing the end of your life before you begin it. You are trying to choose the end of your life before you even begin to live. When you choose to live in ten-second increments, you begin to realize you have choices.

4. Live in the question (instead of the answer).

A question empowers, an answer always dis-empowers. It's a choice to live in the question. When you try to find the answer, it's about trying to get it right. But the right answer eliminates questions from your reality and life. Instead of looking for answers, live in the question.

5. No form, no structure, no significance.

If you are doing form, structure and significance, you are not being conscious. This is because form, structure and significance create limitations. Importance is a significance. When you make anything important, you are owned by it. You have no freedom when you have anything that is important as form, structure or significance in your life. Nothing I own is important to me. No one in my life is important to me. I am grateful for the people in my life, but they not important; they can go away tomorrow. I don't have to hold onto them. I don't have to have them because I am willing for them to be and choose for themselves.

6. No judgment, no discrimination, non discernment.

These are all judgments. If you are doing judgment, you are dead meat. Every judgment eliminates your capacity to perceive anything that does not match it. As soon as you do judgment, you come to a conclusion and cannot see that another choice is available.

7. No drugs of any kind.

If you are doing drugs, you are not choosing consciousness; you are choosing anti-consciousness. This is true for drugs of any kind, including prescription drugs. If you smoke a little pot every once in a while, you are doing drugs. If you use anti-depressants, you are doing drugs. If you smoke a cigarette, you are just trying to numb yourself out. The problem with most drugs is they open the door to entities coming into your body. Once they get in, they start disrupting your physical form and your life. The disadvantage of drugs more than any thing else is not the effect they have on your body. It's the way drugs open the doors to other beings occupying your body.

8. No competition.

Would an infinite being compete with someone else? No. There can't be anybody better than an infinite being. In order to create competition as a reality, you must of necessity create yourself as a finite being. Can anyone truly be competition for you? Or are you the only one of your kind on this planet? The answer, of course, is "You are the only one of your kind on this planet."

9. Do not listen to, tell or buy the story.
The story is just a story; it is not a reality; it is not a truth. The story doesn't mean anything. The story is the way you justify the limitations of your life and your reality. It is the "because." "I would like to do it but...." "It wasn't possible for me to do it because...." These are all things people use to justify why they don't do things in their lives. Getting sucked into the story is listening to it. If you are listening to, telling or buying the story of how pathetic somebody is, or the reason they had to choose drugs, or how awful their life is, or how they have no other choice, or how they can't afford to do this, then you are buying their excuses and justifications as a reality.

10. No Exclusion.
Exclusion is when you exclude another person from coming into your life and being totally present with

you. Exclusion is the way you shut others out. It is not that they shut you out. People will shut you out of their reality, but that doesn't mean you don't include them in yours. People will shut you out of their life, but that doesn't mean you don't include them in yours.

If you would truly have consciousness in your life, the Ten Commandments of Access are the key. Consciousness is actually easier than unconsciousness, but unconsciousness is more familiar, so it seems easier.

Imagine . . .

What would it be like if
the world were a more conscious place?
Would the devastation, wars and difficulties
that are currently going on continue to exist?

The target of Access is to get us to the point
where we are conscious enough to create change
in ourselves, so that our consciousness
will then facilitate or increase the possibility
of changing the trauma, drama and
insanities that are present in life.

What would it be like if you could
change your life enough so that everything
you did was so conscious that others chose to
become more conscious as a result of it?

Consciousness is the opportunity to
eliminate all the created walls of separation.
What will it take for this to become a reality here?

Gary Douglas

Access Energy for Transformation

Contributors

In alphabetical order:

Aubrey B

Chutisa Bowman

Margaret Braunack

Alejandro Perez C

Claudia Cano

John S. Carter

Leena Dillingham

Gary Douglas

Sabrina F

Dr. Dain Heer

Gordon Issom

Ashley L

Denise Levin

Virginia Mealing

Simone Milasas

Claire N

Nancy O'Connor

Simone Phillips

Glenna Rice

Brianna T

Kelsey T

Julie Tuton & Ron Filson

Joy Voeth

♦ ♦ ♦

Edited by Dona Haber

**THE ACCESS BARS CLASS IS A CLASS
FACILITATED BY REGISTERED ACCESS
LEARNING FACILITATORS
WORLD WIDE
Please check out www.accessconsciousness.com for
a list of facilitators and current classes.**

This is a one-day class where you learn a hands-on process and also receive it. This hands-on process has created massive amounts of ease and change for people all over the world. It has created a greater communion within families, assisted students at school and so much more.

There are 32 points or "bars" on the head, including Healing, Body, Sexuality, Money, Control, Aging, Hopes and Dreams, Awareness, Communication, Power, and Creativity, among others. Activating these points by lightly touching them and by allowing the energy to flow through them releases the electrical charge that holds the considerations, thoughts, ideas, beliefs, decisions, emotions or attitudes you have accumulated and stored in any lifetime.

After a "bars" session, the worst thing that can happen is you will feel like you had a great massage. The best thing that can happen is it can change your whole life.

We invite you to attend one of our classes and see what else is possible.

Access True Knowledge Global Foundation
www.accesstrueknowledge.com

The education system as it is currently set up often doesn't validate kids for what they are great at; instead it negates them for what they don't know.

We wish to create school programs or full-time schools that educate kids in a more expansive, dynamic way so they can go beyond the limitations of their current education. We want to create a different possibility.

We would like to design and create a set of schools that will assist kids to access their strengths. Kids know way more than we give them credit for. We would like to fund educational systems that are designed to expand the awareness and possibilities that each individual has. We would like to change the way that the current schooling systems seem to invalidate the creativity and knowing of kids rather than expanding it. In our Access programs and schools, we will also provide a system of education that facilitates kids who are considered disabled, but who actually have incredible abilities.

What would it take to create a place where our kids can be acknowledged for what they know? What would it take for them to realize they are a contribution to everyone around them and to the planet itself? What would it take for them to understand that they have the choice—and the ability—to change the planet?

♦ ♦ ♦

Access Camps
www.theaccesscamp.com

We are developing the Access Camps for Kids worldwide. Please check out the above website for more information about camps being held in the United States, Canada, Australia, New Zealand, Costa Rica and other places.

We have camps for special education kids, adventure camps, body awareness camps, conscious horse conscious rider camps and lots more.

◆ ◆ ◆

If we truly desire to change the planet, we must step up to being the joy that's possible and become the possibilities that we truly are.